FEED

YOUR FRIENDS

Cas Clarke

Illustrations by
Mike Gordon

VIRGIN

A Virgin Book, published in 1989 by
W. H. Allen & Co. Plc
Sekforde House,
175–9 St. John Street, London, EC1V 4LL

Designed by Pat Craddock

ISBN 0 352 32637 9

Typeset by Rapid Communications Ltd, London

Printed and bound by
Cox & Wyman Ltd, Reading, Berkshire

Feast Your Friends

Contents

With many thanks to Andy,
Claire, Neville, Monique,
Guy, Mandy, Dave and all
the other guinea pigs!

Introduction

Why yet another book on Entertaining? Because to my way of thinking no one has yet produced a foolproof book for the beginner. The inexperienced may lack the expertise of the skilled cook but that does not lessen the will to indulge the age-old pleasure of entertaining – preferably without risk of a coronary brought on by excessive anxiety. Entertaining is an art and although some are naturally more adept than others, with practice anything is possible. An inspirational cook can produce wonderful meals with simple ingredients cooked in simple ways. No cordon bleu skills are needed for this, just a love of good food.

The truth behind the art of entertaining lies not in your ability to cook – although this is what your friends will think – but in the organization behind the scenes, the attention paid to the smallest details. Anyone who thinks that entertaining is just about following a recipe from a cookery book successfully will not make a good host.

There are many aspects to entertaining. Not only must one plan, shop, prepare, cook and serve the meal. Life is never so simple. As everyone who entertains knows, this is when you realize that you really MUST clean the house, when you notice those dirty fingerprints on the paintwork, that there are actually cobwebs in the corners. Then you still have to allow for time to make yourself presentable, feed the cat, and do the hundred and one other things that crop up when you least expect them to. When is the most likely time for your long-lost cousin, last seen heading for Borneo, to phone? Yes, that's right: in those crucial moments when you are half-dressed and trying to put the finishing touches to your elaborate starter. Or you can bet that when you have left everything to the last moment, when you have just sunk into that long-awaited bath, *that's* the day your guests will get the time wrong and arrive an hour early.

Don't think these things don't happen: they do, and they will happen to you, especially when you are least prepared for them. Although you can't prevent the unexpected, it doesn't have to herald a disaster. If you are properly organized you will have more time to deal with the unexpected if it should crop up. Organized hosts are calm hosts, who will have time to spend with their guests and enjoy themselves too – and, after all, that is supposed to be the idea behind the evening.

As with all arts, you cannot immediately become a grand master; start with the basics and work up to greater things. However, when first starting out to entertain, if it is not to be too obvious to your guests that you are a complete and utter beginner, try to develop a certain style to hide the simplicity of your cooking. (Simplicity is a necessity to ensure everything is foolproof.) This is where artful entertainers make their mark. Although the meal may be simplicity itself, the ingenious way in which it is presented will impress your friends so much that they will acclaim you a superb cook.

Thus the aim of this book is to show you how best to utilize your precious time, to plan delicious menus which are easy to cook but sensational to serve. I'll give you helpful hints on what to keep in your kitchen, and crafty ways in which to save both time and money. But more importantly, how to get yourself organized, how to acquire the confidence to tackle any event. The artful entertainer knows that confidence is the main ingredient for success. If you are worried about what is going on in the kitchen, whether the soufflé is going flat, if the sauce is going lumpy, you can't possibly enjoy yourself – and if you don't, neither will your guests. Anxiety is contagious. This book will teach you how to acquire the confidence that will banish all anxiety from your entertaining.

Just one word of warning. Guests. Pick these carefully and you will have marvellous dinner parties. However wonderful the food and presentation are, I'm afraid boring dinner guests always lead to boring dinner parties. Cultivate those who obviously enjoy both your company and your food, who spend the evening enjoying themselves oblivious of the fact that the cat has been at the duck or that your cherished soufflé, which never, never goes wrong, tonight has a deflated air. With the right guests, superb food and the right presentation, there is really no better way to spend an evening. So don't be afraid. Go ahead and send out your invitations. You too can be an artful entertainer.

1. Helpful hints

Organization is the key to success. Like a boy scout you must always 'be prepared'.

So the most important part of giving a dinner party is the planning. If you are to appear cool, calm and collected on the night of the party you will have to have done your homework thoroughly. When you have decided to give a dinner party, this is the sort of routine you should follow.

1. Decide WHY you are holding this dinner party and WHO you are inviting. This should make clear just what sort of dinner party you want to hold, be it formal or informal.

2. Decide on a date and invite guests.

3. Look at the relevant chapter and decide on a menu. Don't forget to include accompaniments.

4. Go through each recipe listing ingredients and amounts needed.
- Halve or multiply amounts depending on guests.
- Include something to nibble with pre-dinner drinks.
- Remember to include after-dinner coffee and mints or chocolates.
- Decide whether you wish to have a cheese course and buy cheeses if appropriate.
- Buy wine and soft drinks.
- What about flowers, candles, etc?

5. Condense list to make shopping list.

6. Go through each recipe you have chosen, deciding how long it will take you to prepare. Then make a time plan.

7. Clean house as necessary.

8. Do shopping.

9. Do as much pre-preparation as possible the night before. Include such things as laying the table.

10. On the night follow your time plan, relax and enjoy yourself.

Things to keep in mind

When you are planning your meals keep certain things in mind, such as. . .

1. Make sure you have picked a balanced menu. You don't want a meal which has cheese in every course or cream in every course. Try to keep a balance between light and rich foods. Keep in mind the appearance of each dish. Try to contrast colours and textures.

2. What cutlery and crockery do you have available? Don't plan a meal where you will need your ramekin dishes for the starter and the dessert. Check you have the right number of knives and forks. You *can* wash up between courses, but it is a hassle.

3. Try to use seasonal food. Not only is it cheaper but it is easier to obtain.

4. When planning menus make sure you don't include recipes which clash in cooking methods. If one recipe calls for using the grill and another the oven you're in trouble if the two are combined in your oven.

5. When deciding on your shopping list, don't just assume that you have something in the house. CHECK. You may have a packet of it in the cupboard, but it may not contain enough for your purpose.

6. When making up your time plan, allow plenty of time for chopping up ingredients. This often takes longer than planned for. Also don't forget to allow time to get yourself ready, and to have a drink with your guests when they first arrive.

7. Read each recipe CAREFULLY to ensure you understand it. Pay special attention to words like 'gently'. If the recipe says 'simmer gently' that is what it means, not boil fiercely! Conversely if it says fry something 'quickly' it doesn't mean put it in a pan and leave it while you do something else. Neither of these actions will produce the desired results.

8. Put some effort into creating a party atmosphere. Even if you do not own a dining table you can create the right sort of impression by buying some flowers and having some lit candles.

9. Buy the best wine you can afford from a reputable source e.g. Oddbins, Sainsbury, Marks and Spencer or other reliable chains.

10. Always supply some soft drinks. Orange juice and sparkling mineral water are the firm favourites.

The well-stocked kitchen

If you have just set up your new home, you are probably still stocking your kitchen. There is no need to buy lots of expensive electric gadgets but you will certainly need some items and others come in very useful when entertaining. My kitchen contains the following.

A large CHOPPING BOARD and some good knives. I manage with just two knives. A large CHOPPING KNIFE and an all-purpose SMALL KNIFE with a serrated edge. I do not have a set of matching designer saucepans. I have a Le Creuset MEDIUM-SIZED SAUCEPAN, a LARGE SAUCEPAN WITH CLOSE-FITTING LID, a MILKPAN, a large FRYING PAN and, a worthy investment, my Le Creuset CASSEROLE DISH. You will also need some other ovenproof dish; I have a Le Creuset GRATIN DISH, but any oval-shaped shallow ovenproof dish will do. You will definitely need a BAKING TRAY, also a ROASTING TIN with or without a trivet. A 12-hole BUN TIN and an 8-inch (20cm) LOOSE-BOTTOMED CAKE TIN will also come in very handy. I would be lost without a set of RAMEKIN dishes, which I use constantly when entertaining.

Every kitchen should have plenty of WOODEN SPOONS, a COLANDER and a swivel-bladed POTATO PEELER. An EGG WHISK – the balloon type – and a GRATER are essential if you don't have a FOOD PROCESSOR. I have two sieves, one LARGE SIEVE and a tiny small mesh METAL SIEVE which I keep especially for custards and fruit sauces. You can do without a ROLLING PIN but it can make life easier. True essentials are KITCHEN SCALES, a MEASURING JUG and a NEST OF MEASURING SPOONS. I have found life a lot simpler since I bought a SALAD SPINNER of the spinning-top variety, and I own a lovely GLASS SALAD BOWL for serving salads in.

I consider the above essential, but that doesn't mean that you have to go out and buy them straight away; just keep them in mind when you're out shopping.

I assume that most households have a FREEZER even if it's only the tiny one on top of the fridge. A MICROWAVE OVEN can also come in useful, especially for cooking vegetables and fish. If you don't own a FOOD PROCESSOR you will need a BLENDER/LIQUIDISER for soups, sauces etc.

Ingredients

If you have ever had any contact with computers you will have heard the acronym GIGO which stands for Garbage In, Garbage Out. It holds true for cooking as well. If you use poor quality ingredients in your cooking you will get poor quality results. Good cooking is based on simple recipes using good quality ingredients. This doesn't mean that you can't take short cuts. If you buy ready boned chicken from a good supplier, you are losing nothing of the quality, you are just saving yourself needless effort.

So when you are out shopping don't skimp on things for your store cupboard. It is worth spending a little more; you will certainly get better results.

My cupboards always hold the following.

A good EXTRA VIRGIN OLIVE OIL, as well as some SUNFLOWER OIL and SESAME OIL. I always have FREE-RANGE EGGS, UNSALTED BUTTER and a STRING OF GARLIC. Whenever I am entertaining I always have some LEMONS and FRESH PARSLEY. I always buy WHOLE BLACK PEPPERCORNS to mill and keep MACE and DRIED FRENCH HERBS, as well as DILL. There are many uses for a good WHOLEGRAIN MUSTARD and a medium-flavoured CURRY PASTE, as well as jars of TOMATO PUREE and cans of CHOPPED TOMATOES. A good WINE VINEGAR is useful as is SWEET CHILLI SAUCE. For anything Chinese SOY SAUCE is indispensable.

Always make sure you have both PLAIN and SELF-RAISING FLOUR in your cupboard. CASTER SUGAR and MUSCOVADO SUGAR are the sugars I use most frequently. I keep BASMATI RICE and different types of PASTA in pretty glass jars on display. To go with pasta dishes I keep a lump of PARMESAN CHEESE in the refrigerator and grate it as necessary.

Anyone nervous of using uncooked eggs in a recipe could try some of the new pasteurized egg products that have recently come on the market. SUPERCOOK EGG WHITE is a particularly good substitute for beaten egg whites.

Cooking terms

I have tried to avoid any cooking terms that the average person wouldn't know.

Cooking is largely a matter of taste; no two people actually cook a dish the same way. You will alter these recipes to your own taste, generally by adding the amount of seasoning that you like. So I have tried to be general in terms of adding items like lemon juice, chopped parsley and other herbs. Sometimes I do specify an amount: you should try the recipe with this amount but that doesn't mean that you can't add a little more if you feel that is what you would prefer.

There are a couple of terms I believe may need explaining. When adding wine to a dish, people will vary enormously in the amounts that they use. So if the dish is not dependent on a specific amount I have used the term a 'splash' of wine to indicate that just a little wine is needed to lift the flavour. I use a 'gurgle' to show where you can be a bit more free-handed. I have to admit I prefer to drink wine rather than impart huge quantities of it to the cooking!

Throughout the book I have used a standard of 1oz = 25 grams. For liquid measurements I use 1 fl oz = 25 ml. These are not exact equivalents, so use one set of measurements or the other.

Oven settings

Description	°C	°F	Gas	Description	°C	°F	Gas
Very cool	110	225	¼	Medium-hot	190	375	5
	120	250	½				
Cool	140	275	1	Hot	200	400	6
	150	300	2		220	425	7
Medium	160	325	3	Very hot	230	450	8
	180	350	4		240	475	9

2. Food for friends

The first thing to do is relax. So what, if, in the excite-
ment of moving into your new home, you have invited
some friends round for a meal. You may never have
cooked or held a dinner party before, you may not
have the foggiest idea what you are going to cook,
how much you should cook, how to cook it or even
if you have enough plates to go round, and resources
may be slim. But as I have said before, relax, help is at
hand: with the aid of this book you can cook as good a
meal as any more experienced host.

Now sit back and think. Who did you actually invite?
First establish the actual number that are coming and
when. This is really a crucial point. If in doubt (how
much did you have to drink last night?) give someone
a ring and check. Okay, now that you are quite certain
both of the numbers and of when you are having this

little dinner party, you can do a little planning. Read through my suggested recipes for such occasions as this and muse over what you would like to cook (or use one of my examples to get you going). So now you have some idea of what you could cook. Check that you haven't put together a really boring menu i.e. cheese in every course. You have? Well, replan the menu and remember to watch out for things like that in the future. Next check out what cutlery and crockery you have. You won't have time to enjoy yourself on the night if you are continuously washing up after each course. Don't forget that it is not always necessary to wash cutlery between the starter and the main course: do as the French do and let each guest wipe their cutlery on a piece of bread. Civilized people, the French. Now is the time to decide whether to eat the first course communally (i.e. put it all in the middle and let people help themselves – the problem being that some will help themselves more than others) or whether to plate it as individual helpings. If money is really tight you could put out a few dishes of crisps and nuts and forget the first course entirely.

To help you decide how to serve the first course you should really decide now on the tone of the evening. Ask yourself some crucial questions. Will the highlight of your friends' evening be whether they can knock back ten bottles of wine, or are they actually interested in the food? Is it to be a really casual affair with everyone dressed down for the occasion and you all sitting on the floor? Or are you interested in trying to put over the idea that although you are poor you still have style?

When you have decided on the intended ambiance (and whether it will suit your guests), you should have more idea how to serve the first course. For instance, if your friends are more interested in the drink than the food, forget the starter and stick out some nuts. If your home still resembles a battle site and there is going to be no place to sit other than the floor, it is silly to attempt anything other than a communal meal. It is still possible to be stylish even if you will all be sitting on the floor. A few candles stuck in wax-decorated wine bottles, and shallow dishes with a few flowers floating in them make all the difference. If you do have a table (and chairs!) you still have the choice of whether to go for a bohemian atmosphere with everything presented as simply as possible, or whether you wish to go for a slightly more up-market tone. This would involve a tablecloth (maybe even two toning tablecloths as you see in fancy restaurants), napkins, candles in proper candle holders and flowers on the table. It would also involve plating the first course. The decision is yours.

By the way, a word about flowers. Flowers do make a lovely addition to any table and you can always obtain some cheaply at a local market. There is no need for any sort of elaborate display, just a few simple flowers in a pretty vase.

So things are really coming along now. You've established who your guests are going to be and when they are expected to arrive. You've decided both what you are going to serve and how to serve it. Now comes what is probably the trickiest part of all, the shopping list and a time plan for the actual preparation and cooking.

It is this stage that will make or break your reputation as a cook. The actual cooking is not so tricky, since with the recipes given here it is extremely difficult to get anything wrong. The most probable disaster that can occur when you are just starting to entertain is that you will get to where a recipe says 'Stir in the stock' or 'Add prawns and fry quickly for 2 minutes' only to find that you didn't buy any stock cubes because you thought you had some in the cupboard, or that you didn't get the prawns in the supermarket because they'd be cheaper in the market – and then you forgot all about them. The other thing that can go wrong on the night is not having a proper time plan, resulting in some things being overcooked because you forgot to put the rice on until everything else was ready. These are the things that nightmares are made of.

To reassure you that ordinary mortals can overcome these obstacles, I have provided some examples of how to prepare a shopping list and time plan for a dinner party. Don't forget that if you get the planning right, there is nothing to worry about: the recipes themselves could be cooked by anybody, however little experience you may have in the kitchen.

Don't forget, also, that your friends won't be expecting the same sort of dinner they would get in a 3-star restaurant. They are coming to have a good time and to see you. So relax, you will be at your best if you have already done all the work and have the time to enjoy yourself with your friends.

Example Menu 1

A group of friends, some vegetarian, are coming round tomorrow night to celebrate your moving into your new home. No problem! There'll be 8 of you altogether and you'll be sitting on the floor – but with this menu, you're well on your way to establishing your reputation as a cook.

Menu for 8
Nibble plate
Vegetarian chilli
Garlic bread
No-cook cake

Shopping list
4oz (100g) unshelled pistachio nuts
8oz (200g) mixed black olives and stuffed green olives
8oz (200g) Gruyère cheese
8oz (200g) unsliced salami
2 French sticks
garlic
12oz (300g) butter
parsley
4 large onions
green pepper
2 courgettes
virgin olive oil
2 x 14-oz (400-g) cans tomatoes
2 x 14-oz (400-g) cans red kidney beans

14-oz (400-g) can chick peas
2 packets Old El Paso chilli seasoning mix
cheese
soured cream
12oz (300g) plain chocolate
coffee
brandy
8oz (200g) Amaretto biscuits
6oz (150g) Maraschino cherries
whipping cream
chocolate flake
2 bottles wine
2 bottles mineral water
coffee, milk, sugar, etc. for after dinner

Time plan: to eat at 9.00 – 9.15

The night before make the no-cook cake (page 45) and leave to chill.

8.00 Leave friends in pub with express orders to turn up at the latest by 8.45 – threaten them that you'll drink all the wine if they don't turn up by this time.
8.10 Prepare nibble plate (page 30).
8.20 Put oven on, prepare garlic bread (page 32).
8.35 Prepare vegetable chilli (page 34).
8.50 Put garlic bread in oven.
9.00 Friends actually appear – give them a drink (I expect you've already got one).
9.05 Turn oven up and leave chilli to simmer gently, start on nibble plate.
9.15 Serve chilli and garlic bread.

Later that evening whip cream and crumble flake to serve with no-cook cake.

Example Menu 2

Okay, so you bumped into some friends at lunchtime and impulsively asked them round for a meal tonight. Don't panic! Nip out to the nearest supermarket (most are open until 8.00pm now) with this shopping list and you'll easily be ready on time.

Menu for 4
Hummus
Tacos
Gâteau

Shopping list

8oz (200g) hummus
garlic
cumin
1 lemon
packet pitta bread
1 large onion
virgin olive oil
12oz (300g) extra lean minced beef
14-oz (400-g) can tomatoes
1 packet Old El Paso chilli seasoning mix

1 packet Old El Paso taco shells (12)
lettuce
cheese
soured cream
1 gâteau – will it defrost in time?
1 bottle red wine
1 bottle white wine
1 bottle mineral water
coffee, milk, sugar, etc. for after dinner

Time plan: to eat at 8.00

6.30   Defrost gâteau and lay table.
6.45   Mix up hummus and quarter the lemon for garnish.
6.55   Shred lettuce, grate cheese, put trimmings in little bowls.
7.05   Prepare taco mixture.
7.25   Put oven on, leave taco mixture to simmer gently.
7.30   Friends arrive – have a drink with them.
7.45   Transfer taco mixture to casserole dish and put in bottom of oven to keep warm; put pitta bread in oven to warm up.
8.00   Cut pitta bread into strips and serve with hummus.
8.15   Heat up taco shells and serve.

When ready serve gâteau.

Example Menu 3

The in-laws have just phoned and said that they will be in your area tomorrow – you took the hint and have invited them for a meal. This menu will show them that you have hidden talents.

Menu for 4
Crudités
Rich beef casserole
Chocolate cheesecake

Shopping list

10floz (300ml) soured cream
4oz (100g) soft cream cheese
2lb (1kg) cream cheese
garlic
chives
2 carrots
green pepper
celery
small cauliflower
1½lb (600g) lean stewing beef, cubed
beef dripping
2 onions
paprika
flour
tomato purée
14-oz (400-g) can tomatoes

1 bottle red wine
1 bottle white wine
cornflour
1 packet tagliatelle
ginger snaps
2oz (50g) butter
8oz (200g) caster sugar
4 eggs
5oz (125g) plain chocolate
1oz (25g) cocoa powder
white chocolate
1 bottle mineral water
coffee, milk, sugar, etc. for after dinner
paper napkins
flowers

Time plan: to eat at 7.30

The night before make chocolate cheesecake (page 42), grate white chocolate and keep in fridge until ready to use.

4.30   Put oven on and prepare casserole (page 40).
5.00   Put casserole in oven and lay table.
       Prepare oneself for arrival of in-laws!
6.30   Prepare crudités (page 32), plate individually and cover with clingfilm to keep fresh.
7.00   In-laws arrive – everybody have a drink.
7.30   Put water on to boil for tagliatelle, sit down to crudités.
7.45   Put tagliatelle in water and finish off casserole.
7.55   Serve casserole.
8.30   Serve cheesecake.

When in-laws have departed delighted at your obvious talents – have a stiff drink!

Now you've seen how easy it is, have a go at creating your own menus. Just decide what you will cook (keeping in mind my warning about balancing the courses) then go to each recipe and write out a shopping list from the ingredients – thinking about how many guests you will have and how you are going to serve each course. To prepare a time plan, look at the method for each recipe and work out how long it will take you to prepare (don't forget that chopping up vegetables can often take longer than you expect it to). You should then be able to work out what will take the longest and what can be done at the last moment. Always try to have everything ready for when your guests arrive – don't forget that it is you they have come to see!

Select your menu from these suggestions

Starters
Guacamole

Grape salad
Nibble plate

Tuscan bread
Tomato and olive
starter
Hummus

Garlic bread
Crudités

Main courses
Pasta and 4-cheese
sauce
Cheese fondue
Paella

Tacos
Vegetarian chilli

Kebabs with spicy
sauce
Risotto Bolognese
Tarragon chicken

Rich beef casserole
Colonial curry
Chicken casserole
Lasagne

Desserts
Kiwi cheesecake

Zabaglione trifle
Chocolate
cheesecake
Pavlova
Strawberry tart

Chocolate pudding

No-cook cake
Gâteaux and
ice-creams

Starters

Guacamole
Serves 4
>   2 ripe avocados (they MUST be ripe)
>   1 clove garlic, crushed or chopped
>   ½ onion, finely chopped
>   juice from ½ small lemon or lime
>   1 teaspoon (5ml) tomato purée
>   1 teaspoon (5ml) chopped fresh coriander leaves or pinch of
>   ground coriander
> *Serve with:*
>   tortilla chips

Mash the avocados then beat in all the remaining ingredients until
smooth. Either pile into a bowl, put the bowl on a large plate and
surround with tortilla chips, or divide between 4 ramekins and
serve each on a small plate surrounded by tortilla chips. If you have
fresh coriander you could use some leaves to garnish each plate.

Grape salad

Serves 4

> *Salad:*
> 6oz (150g) broccoli
> ¼ small Iceberg lettuce, shredded
> 2 kiwi fruit, peeled and sliced
> small bunch of green seedless grapes
> *Dressing:*
> 3 tablespoons (45ml) virgin olive or walnut oil
> 1 tablespoon (15ml) lemon juice
> 1 tablespoon (15ml) clear honey
> 1 tablespoon (15ml) wholegrain mustard
> *Serve with:*
> crusty French bread

Chop off the stems of the broccoli and separate into small florets. Mix with the other salad ingredients. Put the dressing ingredients into a lidded container (a screw-top jar?) and shake well. Pour dressing over salad. Serve in small individual bowls or on small plates. Accompany with crusty French bread to mop up the dressing.

Nibble plate

Serves 4

> 2oz (50g) pistachio nuts, unshelled
> 4oz (100g) mixed black olives and stuffed green olives
> 4oz (100g) Gruyère cheese
> 4oz (100g) salami, unsliced

De-rind the cheese and salami, cut into bite-sized pieces. Put a small bowl in the centre of a large plate (which is for the pistachio shells and olive stones) and arrange the 4 groups of nibbles around the bowl.

Tuscan bread
Serves 4

Pre-heat oven to 180°C/350°F/Gas 4

    1 French stick
    4 cloves garlic, peeled
    virgin olive oil

Slice the bread into rounds about ¾ inch (2cm) thick. Bake for 5-10 minutes in the bottom of the oven until bread has dried out and become crisp. Serve the bread warm with the garlic cloves cut in half and a little oil in a small bowl. Each guest should take a piece of bread and rub it with the cut side of a garlic clove: they should then take a small spoonful of oil and trickle a little of the oil over the bread. Make sure that your guests understand that they only need a little oil on their bread or you will have oil everywhere!

Tomato and olive starter
Serves 4

    Salad:
    4oz (100g) large black olives
    4 large tomatoes, thinly sliced
    1 tablespoon (15ml) fresh basil, chopped
    Dressing:
    3 tablespoons (45ml) virgin olive oil
    2 teaspoons (10ml) white wine
    1 teaspoon (5ml) lemon juice
    1 clove garlic, crushed or chopped
    Serve with:
    crusty French bread

De-stone the olives and cut each into 2 or 3 parts. (This always takes longer than you think it is going to!) On small plates arrange a row of olives (skin side up) across the centre of the plate. Arrange a row of tomato slices on each side of the olives. Mix the dressing ingredients together and then pour over the tomatoes and olives. Sprinkle the basil on top and serve with the bread to mop up the dressing.

Hummus
Serves 4
   8oz (200g) hummus
   1 clove garlic, crushed or chopped
   1 teaspoon (5ml) ground cumin
   1 lemon
   Serve with:
   pitta bread
To your shop-bought hummus add the garlic and cumin, mix well. Quarter the lemon and use to garnish the hummus which can be piled in a dish or served individually in ramekins, or on little dishes. Serve with the pitta bread which should be hot and cut into strips.

Garlic bread
Serves 4-6   *Pre-heat oven to 160°C/325°F/Gas 3*
   1 French stick
   6oz (150g) softened butter
   2 cloves garlic, crushed or chopped
   1 tablespoon (15ml) chopped parsley
Cut the bread into thick slices without completely separating each slice. Cream the butter with the garlic and parsley, use to spread between each slice. Wrap loosely in kitchen foil and bake for 15 minutes. Raise the temperature to 220°C/425°F/Gas 7, fold back the foil to expose the bread and bake for a further 10 minutes or until crisp.

Crudités
Serves 4
   Dip:
   5floz (125ml) soured cream
   4oz (100g) soft cream cheese
   1 clove garlic, crushed or chopped
   2 tablespoons (30ml) chopped chives
   Vegetables:
   2 carrots, cut into strips
   1 green pepper, seeded and cut into strips
   2 celery stalks, trimmed and cut into strips
   ½ small cauliflower, broken into florets
Mix all the dip ingredients together and leave to chill. When you have prepared the vegetables the crudités can be served either as a platter or in individual portions. Either pile the dip into a bowl and place on a large plate, surrounding with the vegetables, or divide the dip between 4 ramekins and serve each on a small plate surrounded by a mixture of the vegetables.

Main courses

Pasta and 4-cheese sauce
Serves 4
>3oz (75g) butter
>2 tablespoons (30ml) flour
>8floz (200ml) milk
>12oz (300g) mixed cheeses (e.g. Gouda, Gruyère, Emmenthal, Mozzarella)
>12oz (300g) pasta
>black pepper
>*Serve with:*
>green salad
>crusty French bread

Melt the butter and add the flour, mix well, then gradually add the milk, beating well all the time. Cook the sauce for 1-2 minutes. Grate the cheeses and add to the sauce; stir until cheeses have melted. Cook the pasta as directed on packet. Drain the pasta and add the cheese sauce to it, mix well so that the pasta is covered with the sauce and season with black pepper. I always serve this with a green salad and either French bread or garlic bread. I sometimes also grill some rashers of bacon until very crisp and then crumble them to serve as a side dish of bacon bits.

Cheese fondue
Serves 4
>1 clove garlic, peeled
>10floz (250ml) dry white wine
>12oz (300g) Gruyère cheese, grated
>12oz (300g) Emmenthal cheese, grated
>2 teaspoons (10ml) cornflour
>4 tablespoons (60ml) Kirsch, vodka or gin
>*Serve with:*
>crusty bread, cubed

Rub the inside of the fondue pot with the cut clove of garlic. Heat the wine and add the cheese to it. As it melts, stir well. When the cheese has melted, mix the cornflour with the spirit you are using and add to the fondue mixture, keep stirring as it thickens. Serve bubbling with the cubes of crusty bread: these are speared on fondue forks and then stirred (in a figure of 8) in the cheese fondue. In Switzerland one is expected to forfeit a kiss if one drops a bread cube in the fondue!

Paella

Serves 4-6

> 1 large onion, chopped
> 2 cloves garlic, crushed
> 2oz (50g) butter
> 1 tablespoon (15ml) virgin olive oil
> 12oz (300g) long grain rice
> 14-oz (400-g) can tomatoes
> 30floz (750ml) chicken stock
> 12oz (300g) diced cooked chicken
> 6oz (150g) shelled prawns
> 3oz (75g) peas, cooked
> 1 chorizo sausage, sliced
> *Garnish:* unshelled prawns and cooked mussels in their shells (see moules marinière (page 55) for how to cook mussels)
> *Serve with:*
> garlic bread

Fry the onion and garlic in the oil and butter until beginning to brown, stir in the rice and cook until translucent. Add the tomatoes and mix well. Now stir in the stock and chicken. Simmer for 20 minutes or until the liquid is nearly absorbed, finally stir in the rest of the ingredients. Heat through until all liquid has gone and serve immediately garnished with unshelled prawns and cooked mussels accompanied with garlic bread.

Vegetarian chilli

Serves 4-6

> 2 large onions, chopped
> 2 cloves garlic, crushed
> ½ green pepper, chopped
> 1 courgette, halved and sliced
> 1 tablespoon (15ml) virgin olive oil
> 14-oz (400-g) can tomatoes
> 14-oz (400-g) can red kidney beans
> 7-oz (200-g) can chick peas
> 1 packet Old El Paso chilli seasoning mix
> *Serve with:*
> crusty bread
> grated cheese
> soured cream

Fry onion and garlic in oil until just beginning to brown, add remaining ingredients, cover and simmer for 10-15 minutes to infuse the flavours. Serve in small bowls with the suggested trimmings.

Tacos
Serves 4   *Pre-heat oven to 160°C/325°F/Gas 3*

1 large onion, chopped
2 cloves garlic, crushed
1 tablespoon (15ml) virgin olive oil
12oz (300g) extra lean minced beef
14-oz (400-g) can tomatoes
1 packet Old El Paso chilli seasoning mix
1 packet (12) Old El Paso taco shells
Serve with:
shredded lettuce
grated cheese
soured cream

Fry the onion and garlic in the oil until just beginning to brown, add the minced beef and brown also. Now add the canned tomatoes and seasoning mix, cover and simmer for 10-15 minutes to cook the minced beef. The taco shells can be heated by microwaving for 1 minute or baking in the pre-heated oven for 2-3 minutes. To serve, distribute the seasoned beef between the taco shells and serve with the suggested trimmings. Old El Paso also do a taco sauce which can be served with this; if serving the sauce as well I would add a small salad of sliced avocados. Incidentally you may be wondering why Old El Paso? Because for years I have been researching the ultimate chilli recipe but can find no better seasoning than this chilli seasoning mix. It is also recommended by my brother Desmond who has actually been to Mexico; he gives it 8 out of 10 for authenticity. My case rests!

Kebabs with spicy sauce
Serves 4

    1½lb (600g) leg of lamb, boned and cubed
    2 onions, quartered
    1 green pepper, seeded and cut into squares
    4 tablespoons (60ml) virgin olive oil
    2 tablespoons (30ml) red wine
    1 tablespoon (15ml) clear honey
    1 tablespoon (15ml) tarragon, chopped
    Sauce:
    2 teaspoons (10ml) mild curry powder
    1 teaspoon (5ml) sweet chilli sauce
    2 teaspoons (10ml) tomato purée
    2 teaspoons (10ml) virgin olive oil
    1 tablespoon (15ml) dry vermouth
    5floz (125ml) double cream
    Serve with:
    watercress
    brown rice

Marinate the lamb, onion and pepper in the oil, wine, honey and tarragon for at least 8 hours or overnight. To cook, thread pieces of lamb, onion and pepper onto skewers, cook under a hot grill for 10 minutes, turning frequently and basting with marinade if necessary to stop drying up. To make the sauce mix the curry powder and sweet chilli sauce with the tomato purée and the oil. Next mix in the vermouth and gradually stir in the cream. When the sauce is mixed, heat gently until it is warmed through and serve with the kebabs and brown rice. Garnish each plate with a small bunch of watercress.

Colonial curry
Serves 4-6   *Pre-heat oven to 160°C/325°F/Gas 3*

    2lb (800g) lean stewing steak, cubed
    2oz (50g) plain flour
    2 tablespoons (30ml) curry powder
    4oz (100g) butter
    1 tablespoon (15ml) tomato purée
    10floz (250ml) water
    Serve with:
    basmati rice
    chopped bananas
    mango chutney
    grated coconut
    cubed cucumber mixed with plain yoghurt

Toss the beef in the flour and curry powder. Fry in the butter until brown, add the tomato purée and mix well. Transfer to a casserole dish and add the water. Cover and cook in the pre-heated oven for 1½-2 hours or until meat is cooked. Serve on a bed of basmati rice. The trimmings should be piled into little bowls and handed round to the guests.

Risotto Bolognese
Serves 4-8

      1 onion, chopped
      2 cloves garlic, crushed
      1 tablespoon (15ml) virgin olive oil
      1lb (400g) extra lean minced beef
      2 bacon steaks, cubed
      2 tablespoons (30ml) tomato purée
      12floz (300ml) water
      4floz (100ml) red wine
      2 teaspoons (10ml) Italian seasoning
      1lb (400g) risotto rice (arborio)
      2oz (50g) butter
      1½ pints (750ml) stock
      Serve with:
      Parmesan cheese

Fry the onion and garlic in the oil until just beginning to brown. Add minced beef, bacon, tomato purée and water. Simmer 10 minutes and then add wine and seasoning before simmering for a further 10 minutes. Meanwhile fry the rice in the butter until rice is translucent. Add a third of the stock and boil briskly until stock is absorbed. Add another third of stock and cook again until stock is absorbed. Add the last third of stock and cook until liquid is nearly absorbed. Mix the Bolognese with the rice and serve with grated Parmesan. The basic mixture can be easily stretched by serving a green salad and garlic bread with it. If using the recipe from the starter section for grape salad (page 30) substitute 1 avocado for the kiwi fruit and grapes.

Chicken casserole

Serves 4 *Pre-heat oven to 180°C/350°F/Gas 4*

    4 chicken portions
    2oz (50g) butter
    1 tablespoon (15ml) virgin olive oil
    1 onion, chopped
    2 cloves garlic, crushed
    2 tablespoons (30ml) plain flour
    15floz (375ml) chicken stock
    4 tablespoons (60ml) white wine
    4 tablespoons (60ml) tomato purée
    ½ teaspoon (3ml) mixed herbs
    black pepper
    2 tablespoons (30ml) double cream
    Serve with:
    rice

Fry chicken in butter and oil until brown. Transfer to a casserole dish. Fry the onion and garlic until brown. Stir in the flour and mix well. Add stock, wine, tomato purée, herbs and pepper. Bring to the boil and then pour over the chicken. Cook in the pre-heated oven for 1¼ hours. Before serving stir in the double cream.

I have had to wait many years to get this recipe from my mother. Once you have tried it, you will realize why I persevered: it is the richest, nicest chicken casserole I have ever tasted.

Lasagne

Serves 6 *Pre-heat oven to 180°C/350°F/Gas 4*

    2 onions, chopped
    2 cloves garlic, crushed or chopped
    1 tablespoon (15ml) virgin olive oil
    1lb (400g) lean minced beef
    2 tablespoons (30ml) tomato purée
    14-oz (400-g) can chopped tomatoes
    gurgle of red wine
    sprinkling of Italian herbs
    9 sheets no-cook lasagne
    1 pint (500ml) cheese sauce (page 155)
    2 tablespoons (30ml) grated Parmesan cheese
    Serve with:
    green salad

Fry onion and garlic in oil. Add mince and fry until brown. Add tomato purée, tomatoes, wine and herbs. Simmer gently for 15 minutes. In a greased ovenproof dish put a layer of meat sauce.

Cover with 3 sheets of lasagne. Cover with a third of the cheese sauce. Put another layer of meat sauce on this. Cover with another 3 sheets of lasagne and another third of the cheese sauce. Put a final layer of meat sauce on this and cover with the last 3 sheets of lasagne and a final coat of cheese sauce. Sprinkle with Parmesan cheese and bake in the pre-heated oven for 30-40 minutes until brown.

Tarragon chicken
Serves 4   *Pre-heat oven to 180°C/350°F/Gas 4*

    1 large onion, chopped
    8oz (200g) mushrooms, sliced
    2 celery stalks, sliced
    4oz (100g) butter
    4 chicken breasts, skinned and boned
    1 bottle dry white wine
    1 tablespoon (15ml) chopped tarragon
    black pepper
    10floz (250ml) double cream
    Serve with:
    brown rice or new potatoes

Fry the onion, mushroom and celery in half the butter. Cook for about 10 minutes or until very soft. Add the rest of the butter and the chicken and cook until just beginning to brown. Now put the vegetables and the chicken pieces in a casserole dish. Add the wine and the tarragon and season with black pepper. Cook in the pre-heated oven for 1¼ hours. Just before serving stir in the cream. This is a truly wonderful dish but I do recommend that you keep it for your more alcoholic friends!

Rich beef casserole

Serves 4   *Pre-heat oven to 150°C/300°F/Gas 2*

1½lb (600g) lean stewing beef, cubed
2 tablespoons (30ml) beef dripping
2 onions, chopped
2 cloves garlic, crushed
1 tablespoon (15ml) paprika
1 tablespoon (15ml) flour
4 tablespoons (60ml) tomato purée
14-oz (400-g) can consommé
10floz (250ml) red wine
2 teaspoons (10ml) cornflour
5floz (125ml) soured cream
Serve with:
tagliatelle

Fry the beef in the dripping until browned. Remove to a casserole dish and fry the onion and garlic until just beginning to brown. Add the paprika, flour and tomato purée, mix well. Add a little of the consommé so that you have a sauce, transfer the vegetables and the sauce to the casserole dish. Add the rest of the consommé and the red wine. Cover and cook for 2-3 hours in the pre-heated oven. When the meat is cooked, remove the meat with a slotted spoon and transfer the sauce to a saucepan. Mix the cornflour with a little water and add to the saucepan, bring to the boil and thicken the sauce. Now add the meat and stir well. Take off the heat and add the soured cream before serving.

Kiwi cheesecake
Serves 4-8
> Base:
> 2oz (50g) butter, melted
> 4oz (100g) digestive biscuits, crumbed
> 1oz (25g) soft brown sugar
> pinch cinnamon
> *Filling:*
> 1lb (400g) curd cheese
> 2oz (50g) caster sugar
> grated rind and juice of 2 oranges
> 8floz (200ml) single cream
> ½oz (15g) gelatine
> 3 tablespoons (45ml) cold water
> *To decorate:*
> 3 kiwi fruit, sliced
> whipped cream

Mix the base ingredients together and press firmly into the bottom of an 8-inch (20cm) loose-bottomed cake tin. Press down and chill for 20 minutes. Meanwhile beat the cheese, sugar and orange rind together until smooth. Strain the orange juice and add to the mixture. Gradually stir in the cream. Gently heat the gelatine in the water until dissolved (or dissolve according to instructions on gelatine package), then stir into the cheese mixture. Pour on to the prepared base. Chill in the refrigerator until set. To serve, remove from the tin and decorate with the sliced kiwi fruit and whipped cream.

Zabaglione trifle

Serves 4

> 4 trifle sponges
> 4 tablespoons (60ml) orange juice
> 1 banana, sliced
> 1 nectarine, stoned and sliced
> 1 satsuma, peeled and segmented
> small bunch of seedless white grapes
> 4 egg yolks
> 4oz (100g) caster sugar
> 4 tablespoons (60ml) marsala or sherry
> 5floz (125ml) double cream, whipped
> *To decorate:*
> toasted flaked almonds

Slice each sponge into halves and use to line the bottom of a serving dish or 4 individual dessert bowls. Moisten sponge with the orange juice. Layer the fruits over the sponges. Make the zabaglione by whisking together the egg yolks and sugar in a bowl suspended over a saucepan of boiling water, whisk until mixture thickens. Remove from heat and cool. When egg mixture is cool add the marsala or sherry and then gently mix in the cream. Spoon the zabaglione over the fruit and leave to chill. Sprinkle with some flaked almonds which have been grilled for a few minutes until brown (watch very carefully as they burn easily!).

Chocolate cheesecake

Serves 8   *Pre-heat oven to 180°C/350°F/Gas 4*

> *Base:*
> 4oz (100g) ginger snaps, crushed
> 2oz (50g) butter, melted
> *Filling:*
> 2lb (800g) cream cheese
> 8oz (200g) caster sugar
> 4 eggs
> 5oz (125g) plain chocolate
> 1oz (25g) cocoa powder
> *To decorate:*
> grated white chocolate

Mix the base ingredients together and use to cover the bottom of a greased 8-inch (20cm) loose-bottomed cake tin. Press down and chill for 20 minutes. Beat the cream cheese until it is creamy (an electric whisk is best for this). Mix in the sugar and then gradually add the eggs whisking well all the time. Melt the chocolate and mix with the cocoa powder, then add this to the cheesecake mixture. Pour the mixture on to the prepared base. Bake in the pre-heated oven for 1 hour. Cool and then cover and refrigerate overnight. Remove from tin and serve sprinkled with grated white chocolate.

Chocolate pudding
Serves 4-8

2oz (50g) cornflour
1 pint (600ml) milk
10oz (250g) plain chocolate
3oz (75g) caster sugar
½ teaspoon (3ml) vanilla essence
To decorate:
whipped cream
grated chocolate

Oil a 2-pint (1.2 litre) pudding basin and leave upside down to drain off excess oil. Mix cornflour to a paste with a little of the milk. Gently heat the remaining milk, chocolate and sugar until the chocolate has melted. Pour this on to the cornflour paste and mix well. Return to the heat and stir until mixture boils and thickens. Remove from heat and add vanilla essence. Pour into the basin, cover and chill until pudding sets. To serve: loosen edges and invert on the serving plate, cover with the whipped cream and grated chocolate. (This is not an elegant dessert – it wobbles! But it is delicious.)

Strawberry tart

Serves 4-8   *Pre-heat oven to 220°C/425°F/Gas 7*

        12oz (300g) puff pastry
        2oz (50g) plain chocolate
        2 teaspoons (10ml) oil
        10floz (250ml) double cream
        1 tablespoon (15ml) brandy
        1lb (400g) strawberries, hulled and sliced
        8oz (200g) strawberry jam
        1 teaspoon (5ml) brandy

Defrost the pastry if frozen. Roll out the pastry to a round the same size as the plate you will be serving it on; 2 inches (5cm) from the edge make a cut and continue this cut around the inside of the pastry circle, always keeping 2 inches (5cm) from the edge. When you have completed the circle, lift the border you have just cut whole from the pastry circle. Roll out the pastry circle to the size it was before. Wet the edges and then position the border that you cut out on top of the edges of the circle. Prick the base all over with a fork. Melt the chocolate and the oil together, then, using a pastry brush, cover the pastry base with the chocolate mixture. Be careful to keep the chocolate away from the edge of the pastry. Bake in the pre-heated oven for 15 minutes or until the edges have puffed up. Leave until completely cool. Whisk the cream and tablespoon of brandy until thick, and use to cover the base. Next cover with the sliced fruit. Heat the jam gently with the teaspoon of brandy, sieve to remove any fruit and then use to glaze the tart. Chill until ready to serve.

Pavlova

Serves 4

        2 egg whites
        4oz (100g) caster sugar
        1 teaspoon (5ml) cornflour
        ½ teaspoon (3ml) vinegar
        1 teaspoon (5ml) vanilla essence
        To decorate:
        whipped cream
        fresh fruit
        icing sugar

Whisk the egg whites until stiff, then add half the sugar, and whisk again until mixture is thick and shiny. Whisk in the remaining sugar and remaining ingredients. Cover a baking tray with baking parchment, brush with oil and dust with icing sugar. Spread the pavlova mixture in a round in the middle of the tray; it should be about 1 inch (3cm) high. Bake at 140°C/275°F/Gas 1 for 1 hour. It should now be a pale biscuit colour. Place it upside down on the serving dish and remove the baking parchment. The middle should sink slightly giving a hollow which can be filled with any combination of prepared fresh fruit. Cream can be piped around the sides. I particularly like strawberries and kiwi fruit in this but there are many other popular combinations, such as summer berries, bananas and grapes, black cherries soaked in kirsch and my other half's favourite, raspberries with a strawberry and brandy purée.

No-cook cake
Serves 4-8

    12oz (300g) plain chocolate
    4 tablespoons (60ml) strong black coffee
    4 tablespoons (60ml) brandy
    8oz (200g) Amaretto biscuits, broken
    6oz (150g) Maraschino cherries
    To decorate:
    whipped cream
    grated chocolate

Gently heat the chocolate and coffee together until chocolate melts. Remove from the heat and add remaining ingredients. Mix thoroughly. Turn into a greased 8-inch (20cm) loose-bottomed cake tin. Smooth the top and chill overnight. To serve remove from the tin and cover with cream and grated chocolate.

Gateaux and ice creams _____

There are numerous gateaux and ice creams on the market which are very good and suitable for a dinner-party dessert. You should always pick a reputable make and follow the instructions on the packet to serve. If it says defrost for 4 hours, it means defrost for *4 hours*, not 30 minutes!

It is sometimes nice to serve a bought dessert with some whipped cream which has had brandy or a liqueur whipped in with it; it just adds a little home-made touch to it. Please do not pretend that you made the dessert yourself: your friends will not believe you and you will besmirch your reputation as a cook. If you are serving a bought dessert it is not because you couldn't make something equally nice, but because you are pushed for time and yet still want something wicked to end your meal.

3. Seduction suppers

A meal for two can be a very special occasion. Whether you are cooking for the love of your life, or for the person you hope will become the love of your life, this meal is a symbol. It is an offering of love and therefore great things are expected of it. A seduction supper should be simple. (The best must be champagne and caviar – although this does make your intentions rather obvious!) It should also be light; any stodge is completely out. The whole effort has been a waste if you both fall asleep afterwards.

Of course if this is your first attempt at cooking something for your intended (especially if the victim is unaware of your intentions) you will be nervous. Don't worry, this is natural and even a complete beginner can cook these meals.

However it is the established couple that these recipes are really for. There is no better way to keep the magic in your relationship than to indulge periodically in a seduction supper. Although it is nice to celebrate a birthday or anniversary in this manner, I wholeheartedly recommend that these recipes are not kept purely for such occasions.

Everyone likes to be pampered, and to have a lovely meal prepared for you does make you feel rather special. You may come home tired from a hard day's work, with no other thought in your mind than putting your feet up by the telly. However, an inviting aroma as you walk through the door, a relaxing bath as the last touches are put to the meal and that pre-dinner drink will surely lead your thoughts to more enjoyable prospects for the evening!

Example Menu 1

Your other half 'phoned you from work earlier and moaned that he or she wouldn't be home until 8.00 (or even later) and you know this will make for a grumpy evening. As the shops are open late tonight, you decide to change all that by cooking a special meal.

Firstly decide on the menu – opting for recipes that don't call for precise timing (bearing that 'later' in mind!). Then run through the recipes and make out a shopping list – not forgetting what you will be serving with the main course and coffee afterwards. When that's all done sit down with a cuppa and work out your time plan bearing in mind you'll be eating about 8.30-9.00. So. . .

Menu for 2
Avocado and chilli-dressed prawns
Ham-wrapped chicken, tagliatelle, green salad
Chocolates

Shopping list

virgin olive oil
tomato purée
chilli powder
2oz (50g) shelled prawns
1 ripe avocado
1 lemon
2 boned and skinned chicken breasts
2 large slices Parma ham
2oz (50g) Gruyère cheese
paprika
unsalted butter
chicken stock cubes
dry white wine
small carton double cream

tagliatelle
lettuce
cress
cucumber
kiwi fruit
green pepper
French dressing
chocolates
fresh coffee beans, sugar etc. for after dinner
(There'll be some cream left so no need for extra milk for coffee.)
1 bottle wine

Time plan: to eat at 8.30 (or later!)

7.45 Prepare green salad, cover and keep in refrigerator.
8.00 (or when other half returns from work)
Put oven on to heat up.
Start preparing ham-wrapped chicken (page 57).
8.25 (or 5 minutes before you wish to eat)
Put chicken in oven.
Prepare avocado and chilli-dressed prawns (page 56).
8.30 (or when ready to eat)
Put water on to boil for tagliatelle.
Serve avocado and prawns.
8.40 (or 15 minutes before main course)
Put tagliatelle on to cook.
Dress salad.
8.55 (or when ready to eat main course)
Serve main course and follow with coffee and chocolates when ready.

Example Menu 2

A tall dark and handsome stranger has crossed your path. You've enticed him to your home with tales of your culinary skills. But the proof of the pudding is in the eating.

You want to impress your guest but you certainly don't want either of you to fall asleep after the meal!

Menu for 2
Melon with port
Peppered steak, new potatoes, petits pois
Chocolate rum mousse

Shopping list

1 small ogen melon
miniature port
2 fillet steaks
butter
black peppercorns
wholegrain mustard
small carton soured cream
new potatoes
frozen petits pois

2oz (50g) plain chocolate
2 eggs
ginger cake
miniature dark rum
chocolate flake
coffee, milk, sugar etc. for after
    dinner
1 bottle red wine
candles!

Time plan: to eat at 8.00

Before you start make sure you are ready, the table is laid (the candles ready to be lit, the wine opened) – and don't forget to wear an apron while cooking.

6.30　Make chocolate rum mousse (page 63).
6.50　Prepare melon with port (page 56).
7.00　Prepare new potatoes and leave covered with water.
　　　Have a drink with your guest when he arrives.
8.00　Put water on to boil for vegetables.
　　　Serve melon with port.
8.15　Put potatoes on to cook.
　　　Start peppered steaks (page 59).
　　　When steaks are simmering put petits pois on to cook.
　　　Actual serving time will depend on how your guest likes his
　　　steak cooked.

Serve chocolate rum mousse when appetites dictate.

Example Menu 3

It's that annual occasion – your anniversary dinner. This is when you pull all the stops out in an effort to remind your partner why you were picked! When the lights are low, the music softly playing and the wine flowing freely, this is the perfect way to end your day.

Menu for 2
Artichokes with melted butter
Scampi Provençale, rice, mixed salad
Lemon syllabub

Shopping list

2 globe artichokes
butter
olive oil
small onion
garlic
7-oz (200-g) can chopped tomatoes
1 bottle dry white wine
tomato purée
Italian herbs
8oz (200g) shelled scampi
white long-grain rice

lettuce
small red cabbage
carrot
cherry tomatoes
French dressing
1 lemon
small carton double cream
icing sugar
1 egg
coffee, milk, sugar etc. for after dinner
liqueur chocolates

Time plan: to eat at 8.00

6.15   Prepare lemon syllabub (page 64).
6.30   Prepare mixed salad, cover and leave in refrigerator.
         Now allow some time to set the table and put the finishing touches to yourself!
7.15   Prepare artichokes and cook.
         Have a drink with your partner.
7.55   Drain artichokes and melt butter to serve with them.
8.00   Serve artichokes.
8.15   Put rice on to cook.
8.20   Cook scampi Provençale (page 61).
8.45   Dress salad and serve main course.

Follow with dessert when appetites dictate.

Select your menu from these suggestions

Starters	Main courses	Desserts
Prawn cocktail	Chicken with garlic cream	Chocolate rum mousse
Crevettes in lime dressing	Ham-wrapped chicken	Fresh fruit salad
Oysters	Chicken Caribbean	Lemon syllabub
Moules marinière	Peppered steak	Fruit brulée
Avocado and chilli-dressed prawns	Mushroom-stuffed steak	Strawberry cream
Stilton pâté	Grilled steaks with herb butter	Cherries in red wine
Artichokes	Fish steaks with herbs	Fruit fool
Melon with port	Stuffed trout	Chocolates
	Scampi Provençale	
	Mushroom-stuffed pasta	
	Baked nut-topped avocados	
	Avocado and Stilton puffs	

Starters

Prawn cocktail
Serves 2

> lettuce leaves, shredded
> 2oz (50g) shelled prawns
> 2 tablespoons (30ml) mayonnaise
> 1 teaspoon (5ml) tomato purée
> few drops Worcestershire sauce
> paprika
> *To garnish:*
> 2 lemon quarters

On small plates or glass dishes arrange the shredded lettuce leaves. Next mix the mayonnaise and tomato purée together and add Worcestershire sauce to taste. Mix this sauce with the prawns and then pile the prawns on top of the lettuce. Sprinkle some paprika over them and garnish with the lemon quarters.

Crevettes in lime dressing
Serves 2

> 1oz (25g) unsalted butter
> 1 clove garlic, crushed or chopped
> 1 lime, grated rind and juice
> sprinkling of ground ginger
> 4 crevettes
> *To decorate:*
> lime quarters
> *Serve with:*
> French bread

Melt the butter and add garlic, ½-teaspoon lime rind, lime juice, ginger and crevettes. Heat gently and then serve on small plates garnished with lime quarters and serve with slices of French bread to mop up the delicious dressing.

Oysters
Serves 2

> 1 dozen oysters
> *Serve with:*
> lemon quarters

Open the oysters with a knife just before serving by pushing a short, strong knife blade into the hinge and pressing the shells apart. Break off and discard the flatter shell and serve each oyster on its remaining shell. This looks very impressive if you can serve the oysters on a bed of cracked ice garnished with the lemon quarters.

If you have not eaten oysters before, this is what you do. The oyster is sprinkled with lemon juice and then, taking the shell in one hand, you slip the oyster into your mouth. They have a reputation as aphrodisiacs – so may be a good choice for a seduction supper!

Moules marinière
Serves 2

    1¾ pints (1 litre) fresh mussels in shells
    gurgle of dry white wine
    knob of butter
    chopped parsley
    chopped onion or chives
    Serve with:
    crusty French bread

Soak the mussels in cold water, scrub well and pull away the beards. Discard any that are not tightly closed. Give a last clean under cold running water and then put with other ingredients in a large saucepan. Cook covered over a gentle heat for a few minutes until all have opened. Divide between 2 large soup bowls and pour the cooking liquor over the open mussels. The correct way to eat mussels is to eat your first mussel and then use the discarded shell to pick the next mussel from its shell. You should provide a large bowl for the empty shells. The crusty bread should be used to mop up the delicious juices.

By the way this is not a recipe for the squeamish as I find that the noise of air escaping from the shells as the mussels cook sounds like little squeals! One way around this is to cook them for a couple of minutes in the microwave; as soon as the shells open they are ready – and this way you don't hear any noises!

Artichokes
Serves 2

    2 globe artichokes
    Serve with:
    melted butter

Trim the leaves and the base so that each artichoke will stand upright. Boil for 30-40 minutes or until a leaf will pull away easily. Drain upside down while melting your butter. Serve each artichoke in a pool of melted butter.

    To eat: a leaf is pulled out and its base dipped in the butter; then the base is sucked from the leaf, which is then discarded. When the bottom is reached the hairy 'choke' is carefully removed and the 'heart' eaten with a knife and fork.

Avocado and chilli-dressed prawns
Serves 2
> 2 teaspoons (10ml) olive or walnut oil
> 1 tablespoon (15ml) tomato purée
> sprinkling of chilli powder or sweet chilli sauce
> 2oz (50g) shelled prawns
> 1 ripe avocado
> a little lemon juice
> *To garnish:*
> lemon quarters

Mix the oil, purée, chilli and prawns together. Halve the avocado and remove the stone, squeeze a little lemon juice over the surfaces and then fill the hole left by the stone with the chilli-dressed prawns. Serve garnished with the lemon quarters.

Stilton pâté
Serves 2
> 1oz (25g) butter
> 1oz (25g) plain flour
> 8floz (200ml) milk
> 4oz (100g) grated Stilton
> 1 teaspoon mayonnaise
> 1 clove garlic, crushed or chopped
> salt and pepper
> *Serve with:*
> hot toast

Melt the butter and then stir in the flour, cook, stirring for a few minutes and then slowly add the milk over a gentle heat. Continue stirring until boiling and you have a thick sauce. Leave to cool completely. Then add the rest of the ingredients and mix thoroughly. Spoon into individual ramekins and serve chilled with fingers of hot toast.

Melon with port
Serves 2
> 1 small ogen melon
> 2 tablespoons (30ml) port

Cut melon in half and scoop out the seeds. Trim base of each half so that it will stand upright. Pour 1 tablespoon (15ml) port into each half and chill for at least 1 hour before serving.

Main courses _____

Chicken with garlic cream
Serves 2

    2 chicken breasts, skinned and boned
    2oz (50g) garlic flavoured soft cheese
    1oz (25g) unsalted butter
    2 tablespoons (30ml) dry white wine
    1 tablespoon (15ml) double cream
    Serve with:
    green beans, rice

Flatten chicken breasts gently (i.e. with rolling pin) then divide the cheese between the 2 breasts and fold up so that the cheese is completely enclosed; secure with the cocktail sticks. Melt the butter and brown the chicken on all sides. Then add the wine and cream, cover, and simmer very gently for 15 minutes. Serve with the sauce poured over the chicken.

Ham-wrapped chicken
Serves 2   *Pre-heat oven to 180°C/350°F/Gas 4*

    2 chicken breasts, skinned and boned
    2 large slices Parma ham
    2oz (50g) Gruyère cheese, grated
    1oz (25g) unsalted butter
    3 tablespoons (45ml) chicken stock
    3 tablespoons (45ml) dry white wine
    1 tablespoon (15ml) double cream
    sprinkling of paprika
    Serve with:
    tagliatelle
    green salad

Flatten the chicken breasts gently. Then lay each breast on a slice of ham. Sprinkle half the cheese over the 2 breasts. Then roll each packet up with the cheese inside and secure with cocktail sticks. Melt the butter in a frying pan and fry the chicken to seal each side. Put in a small casserole dish. Add the stock and wine to the frying pan and boil until reduced. Pour over the ham-wrapped packets and then pour the cream over. Sprinkle the remaining cheese over and then sprinkle with paprika. Cover and bake in the pre-heated oven for 25-30 minutes. Serve with tagliatelle and a green salad.

Chicken Caribbean
Serves 2

> 2 chicken breasts, skinned and boned
> ½ red pepper
> ½ green pepper
> 1oz (25g) butter
> 1 banana
> 1 teaspoon (5ml) curry paste
> 10floz (250ml) white sauce (page 155)
> 1 tablespoon (15ml) double cream
> *Serve with:*
> mixed vegetables and rice

Dice chicken. Cut peppers into strips, then cut each strip into diamond shapes. Fry chicken and peppers gently in butter until chicken is cooked through. Cut banana into rounds and add to the pan. Next add the curry paste and mix well. Add the white sauce and cream and again mix well. Heat gently to warm through then serve on a bed of vegetable rice.

Peppered steak
Serves 2

1oz (25g) butter
2 fillet or rump steaks
1 teaspoon (5ml) black peppercorns
black pepper
1 teaspoon (5ml) wholegrain mustard
5floz (125ml) soured cream
Serve with:
new potatoes
petits pois

Melt butter and fry steaks quickly on both sides until brown. Turn heat down and add peppercorns, a sprinkling of ground pepper, mustard and cream. If you like your steaks rare cook for only 4 minutes turning once. For medium or well-done steaks cook for 8-12 minutes. Serve with new potatoes and petits pois.

Mushroom stuffed steak
Serves 2

2 thick fillet steaks
2oz (50g) mushrooms, finely sliced
1oz (25g) garlic-flavoured soft cheese
1oz (25g) unsalted butter
2 teaspoons (10ml) wholegrain mustard
10floz (250ml) white sauce (page 155)
Serve with:
petits pois
jacket baked potatoes

Cut a horizontal slit in each steak, mix mushrooms and cheese together and use to fill the slit. Melt butter and cook steaks gently for 5 minutes. Add mustard to the pan and then the white sauce; mix thoroughly. Cook for a further 4 minutes for rare steaks, or 8-12 minutes for medium to well-done steaks. Serve with petits pois and jacket baked potatoes.

Grilled steaks with herb butter
Serves 2
  2 rump steaks
  red wine for marinading
  2oz (50g) butter
  1 tablespoon (15ml) finely chopped fresh parsley
  melted butter
  Serve with:
  mushrooms
  jacket baked potatoes

First marinate the steaks in a little red wine; leave for at least 2 hours. Beat together the butter and parsley. Roll into a tube and cover with clingfilm; chill. Brush the steaks with melted butter and put under a pre-heated grill. Grill on a high heat for 1 minute on each side. Turn the grill down· to a low to medium heat and continue grilling for 4 minutes for rare steaks, 8-12 minutes for medium to well-done steaks. When done remove the clingfilm from the butter and cut into slices. Serve the steaks topped with the butter slices with mushrooms and jacket baked potatoes.

Fish steaks with herbs
Serves 2
  2 tablespoons (30ml) olive oil
  splash of white wine
  juice of 1 lemon
  1 tablespoon (15ml) chopped fresh herbs, rosemary
    or parsley
  2 firm fish steaks (e.g. monkfish)
  1oz (25g) butter
  Serve with:
  green salad
  new potatoes

Mix the oil, wine, lemon juice and herbs together and use to marinate the fish. Leave 1 or 2 hours. Fry the steaks gently in the butter; when flesh is white, add the marinade mixture and simmer for 1 minute. Serve steaks with juices poured over and a green salad and new potatoes.

Stuffed trout
Serves 2   *Pre-heat oven to 180°C/350°F/Gas 4*

    2 tablespoons (30ml) fresh breadcrumbs
    2oz (30ml) white crab meat
    1 tablespoon (15ml) double cream
    sprinkling paprika
    2 rainbow trout, cleaned and boned
    Serve with:
    green beans
    new potatoes

Mix together the breadcrumbs, crab meat, cream and paprika, and use mixture to stuff the trout. Put in a covered casserole dish or wrap in foil. Bake in the pre-heated oven for 20 minutes.

Scampi Provençale
Serves 2

    1 small onion, finely chopped
    1 garlic clove, crushed or chopped
    1 tablespoon (15ml) olive oil
    7-oz (175-g) can chopped tomatoes
    2 tablespoons (30ml) white wine
    1 tablespoon (15ml) tomato purée
    1 tablespoon (15ml) Italian herbs
    8oz (200g) shelled scampi
    Serve with:
    white rice
    side salad

Fry the onion and garlic in oil until soft. Add all remaining ingredients except scampi and simmer quickly until a thickish sauce is formed. Add scampi and cook for a further 8 minutes. Serve on a bed of rice with a side salad.

Baked nut-topped avocados
Serves 2   *Pre-heat oven to 200°C/400°F/Gas 6*

  1 large ripe avocado
  squeeze of lemon juice
  2oz (50g) curd cheese
  1 teaspoon (5ml) dried mixed herbs
  1 tablespoon (15ml) double cream
  1 tablespoon (15ml) fresh breadcrumbs
  1oz (25g) Gruyère cheese, grated
  1oz (25g) shelled walnuts, crumbled
  Serve with:
  new potatoes
  broccoli

Cut the avocado in half and remove stone. Scoop out the flesh and mash well. Mix the lemon juice, curd cheese and herbs together and then blend with the avocado flesh. Use to stuff avocado skins (or use small gratin dishes). Mix cream, breadcrumbs, cheese and walnuts and use to top avocado mixture. Bake for 15 minutes or until just beginning to brown. Serve with new potatoes and broccoli.

Avocado and Stilton puffs
Serves 2   *Pre-heat oven to 200°C/400°F/Gas 6*

  1 ripe avocado
  2oz (50g) Stilton cheese, crumbled
  4oz (100g) puff pastry
  egg yolk
  Serve with:
  new potatoes
  mixed salad or mixed vegetables

Halve the avocado and remove stone. Scoop out flesh and discard skins. Mash the flesh with the Stilton cheese. Roll the pastry out thinly and cut into 4 squares. Divide the avocado mixture between the squares and then fold each square into a triangle. Moisten and seal each edge. Brush with the egg yolk and cook for 20 minutes or until brown. Serve with new potatoes and a mixed salad or mixed vegetables.

Mushroom-stuffed pasta
Serves 2

 8oz (200g) mushrooms, finely chopped
 ½ onion, finely chopped
 3oz (75g) butter
 1 clove garlic, crushed or chopped
 1 teaspoon (5ml) Italian seasoning
 1 tablespoon (15ml) tomato purée
 3oz (75g) penne, or large shell pasta
 splash of white wine
 2 tablespoons (30ml) double cream
 freshly ground black pepper
 Serve with:
 green salad

Fry the mushrooms and onion in 2oz (50g) of the butter. When most of the butter has been absorbed, add the garlic, herbs and tomato purée. Mix well and cook until all the liquid has been absorbed. Put aside to use as stuffing. Cook the pasta as directed on packet. When cooked fill each penne or pasta shell with a little of the stuffing (this is very time-consuming – but it is well worthwhile as the taste is sensational). Next melt the remaining butter and add the stuffed pasta, wine and cream, season with pepper. Heat through gently, stirring carefully. Serve with a green salad.

Desserts ────────────────────────────

Chocolate rum mousse
Serves 2

This recipe is always very popular with both sexes. However if you feel it may be a little too filling for the end of your meal, just make up the mousse and serve it in individual glasses or ramekins.

 2oz (50g) plain chocolate
 2 eggs, separated
 ginger cake
 1 tablespoon (15ml) dark rum
 chocolate flake, crumbled

Melt the chocolate in a bowl over some hot water (or in the microwave if you have one). Whisk the egg whites and beat the yolks. Remove the chocolate from the heat and stir in the egg yolks. Fold in the egg whites. Put a slice of ginger cake into each of 2 serving dishes. Divide the rum between the 2 dishes, then spread the mousse mixture over each slice of cake. Chill in the refrigerator until set. Sprinkle the chocolate flake on top just before serving.

Fresh fruit salad
Serves 2

    1 banana
    1 nectarine
    small bunch seedless grapes
    1 measure Cointreau

Skin and chop the banana. De-stone the nectarine and slice thinly. De-stalk the grapes and mix the fruits together. Marinate in the Cointreau until ready to serve.

Lemon syllabub
Serves 2

    1 lemon, grated rind and juice
    5floz (125ml) double cream, whipped
    1 tablespoon (15ml) dry white wine
    2 teaspoons (10ml) icing sugar
    1 egg white, whisked

Mix together the first 3 ingredients. Whisk until the cream holds its shape. Add the icing sugar and whisk again. Fold in the egg white. Spoon into individual serving glasses and chill.

Fruit brulée
Serves 2

    8oz (200g) soft fruit (blackberries, etc.)
    1 tablespoon (15ml) sugar
    1 tablespoon (15ml) water
    5floz (125ml) double cream
    1oz (25g) brown sugar

Gently stew the fruit with the sugar and water until the juices flow. Divide the fruit between 2 ramekin dishes and chill thoroughly. Divide the cream between the 2 dishes and top with the brown sugar. Grill until the sugar bubbles and browns. Serve immediately.

Strawberry cream
Serves 2

    8oz (200g) fresh strawberries (hulled)
    5floz (125ml) double cream, whipped
    small egg white, stiffly whisked
    1 tablespoon (15ml) caster sugar

Reserve 2 whole strawberries then pulp the rest. Mix with the whipped cream. Fold in the whisked egg white and caster sugar. Pile into 2 small bowls and top each with a whole strawberry.

Cherries in red wine
Serves 2

> 5floz (125ml) red wine
> 1oz (25g) caster sugar
> few drops vanilla essence
> sprinkling of cinnamon (or cinnamon stick)
> 2 cloves
> 8oz (200g) cherries, stoned
> *Serve with:*
> double cream

Put all ingredients into a saucepan and heat until sugar dissolves. Simmer for 5 minutes. Remove the cloves and cinnamon stick if used. Serve warm with cream.

Fruit fool
Serves 2

> 5floz (150ml) full fat yoghurt
> 4oz (100g) dried apricots, soaked overnight
> 1 tablespoon (15ml) apricot brandy

Reserve a tablespoon of yoghurt. Then purée rest of ingredients until smooth. Spoon into individual glasses and swirl a little yoghurt on to the top of each.

Chocolates
These are actually my favourite way to finish a seduction supper. However don't opt for the usual variety-in-a-box. For this occasion you want delicious handmade chocolates. Only buy a small number: for 2 people 4-6 chocolates is ample. You want to tempt the palate, not sicken it!

4. Food to impress

There are certain times when it is ultra-important that
the food is good, company congenial and the atmosphere just right. Probably the occasions that spring
most readily to mind are entertaining your boss or
company clients. Or it might just be the first time you
have invited new friends around, and your relationship
hasn't got to the stage yet where it really doesn't matter what is served up.

These occasions can often become stilted as the hosts cannot behave naturally as they are too worried about everything being 'right'. That is why it is more important than ever to be confident of what you are cooking and to know that everything will turn out right.

I have picked these recipes very carefully. All are very easy to cook but on the other hand they make very grand dinners. I am sure your guests will be both impressed and delighted with the results. But the best thing about them is the confidence that is generated in knowing that nothing can go wrong. This allows you to relax and enjoy yourself, in turn ensuring that your guests enjoy themselves.

When you are trying to impress people you should really push the boat out. I always give my guests something to nibble on while we are having a pre-dinner drink. This helps to break the ice. Often I just put out some assorted nuts but if time is available you could always prepare a few canapés from the selection in the 'parties' chapter (page 127). I also often serve cheese and biscuits at these affairs as an extra course. The British generally prefer the cheese course at the end of the meal, but true sophisticates serve it before the dessert, as the French do. Then to finish off the meal you could serve chocolates, mints or even liqueur chocolates with the coffee.

Another reason for having cheese and perhaps fruit in the house is that it provides an alternative if something disastrous happens to the dessert, such as you dropping it as you take it from the refrigerator, or the cat devouring it when your back is turned. For this reason also I tend to keep a melon in the refrigerator and a bottle of port handy. Just in case something should happen to my starter, then I can quickly make an alternative. If something unforeseen happens to your main course, this is a lot harder to disguise. However if you always keep some pasta and canned smoked oysters in your cupboard, and cream and Parmesan in your refrigerator you can always bung these together in a sauce and call it the speciality dish of the house. Confidence is all!

Anyway, just having these things in the house usually ensures that nothing does go wrong. Confident cooks are not nervous cooks, and disasters strike these people far less often than nervous souls!

And please don't hit the bottle too hard, so that if any quick thinking is needed you have a clear mind capable of solving any problem. Alternatively you could always get rid of the cat!

Example Menu 1

Your company has two visitors from abroad. After they have already spent a week in their hotel enduring the food, you offer to show them some British hospitality – your offer is eagerly snapped up. With this menu you can show them how good British cooking can be.

Menu for 4
Watercress soup
Individual beef Wellingtons
Whisky and walnut parfait

Shopping list
butter
1 onion
2 bunches watercress
vegetable stock cubes
milk
instant potato powder
4 fillet steaks
garlic
2 bottles red wine
4oz (100g) mushrooms
4 sheets ready-rolled puff pastry
4oz (100g) firm meat pâté

10floz (250ml) double cream
eggs
broccoli
baby carrots
soft brown sugar
miniature whisky
3oz (75g) shelled walnut halves
salted nuts to serve before meal
coffee, milk, sugar etc. to serve after dinner
mints

Time plan: to eat at 8.00

The night before make the whisky and walnut parfait. Do any necessary cleaning.

Before you start, make sure the table is laid, the wine opened and that you are ready. Wear an apron while cooking.

6.30   Start preparing vegetables.
6.45   Make watercress soup (page 76): cover to ensure a skin does not form.
7.15   Prepare beef Wellingtons.
7.30   Put beef Wellingtons into refrigerator to chill. Pre-heat oven. Transfer whisky and walnut parfaits from freezer to refrigerator.
       Have a drink with your guests.
7.55   Re-heat soup. Put water on to boil for vegetables.
8.00   Put vegetables on to cook. Put beef Wellingtons into oven. Serve soup.
8.10   Make gravy for beef Wellingtons.
8.15   Serve main course.

When appetites dictate serve the whisky and walnut parfait.

Example Menu 2

You have just started a new job and in an effort to get to know your boss and his or her partner you have invited them to dinner. When you get home panic strikes – what on earth are you going to cook? How about. . .

Menu for 4
Chilled prawn soup
Pigeon breasts with wine sauce
Crème caramel

Shopping list
8oz (200g) unpeeled prawns
fish stock cubes
1 bottle dry white wine
1 bottle red wine
butter
plain flour
5floz (125ml) single cream
tomato purée
8 pigeon breasts or 4 frozen pigeons
beef stock cubes
cornflour
jar of cranberry and port sauce
new potatoes
cabbage
raisins
caster sugar
milk

vanilla essence
eggs
8oz (200g) mixed berries
nuts to serve before dinner
coffee, milk, sugar etc. for after dinner
handmade chocolates

Time plan: to eat at 8.00

The night before make the crème caramel and the prawn soup. Defrost pigeons if necessary. Clean the house.

On the night, make sure you are ready and have laid the table and opened the wine before you start.

6.45 Prepare vegetables and remove breasts from pigeons if using whole pigeons.
7.15 Make pigeon breasts in wine sauce and leave in cool oven. Have a drink with your guests.
7.55 Finish preparing soup. Put water on to boil for vegetables.
8.00 Put vegetables on to cook. Serve soup.
8.15 Serve main course.

Serve dessert when guests are ready for it.

Example Menu 3

Your other half casually mentions that the boss and partner have been invited to dinner – and they are veggies! No problems with this gourmet vegetarian dinner.

Menu for 4
Avocado with raspberry dressing
Classic cheese soufflé
Walnut and honey tart

Shopping list

1 punnet fresh raspberries
2 bottles German white wine
2 ripe but still firm avocados
unsalted butter
plain flour
cornflour
milk
3oz (75g) Gruyère cheese
7 eggs
Parmesan cheese
wholegrain mustard
new potatoes
broccoli

8oz (200g) ready-made short-crust pastry
soft brown sugar
clear honey
vanilla essence
4oz (100g) shelled walnut halves
5floz (125ml) single cream
5floz (125ml) double cream
assorted nuts to serve before dinner
coffee, milk, sugar etc. for after dinner
liqueur chocolates

Time plan: to eat at 8.00

The night before prepare the walnut and honey tart. Prepare the raspberry dressing and leave in refrigerator. You have cleaned the house, haven't you?

Table laid and wine opened, you are ready to start.

7.00   Prepare vegetables, butter soufflé dish. Pre-whisk egg whites. Grate cheeses.
       Have drink with guests.
7.45   Prepare soufflé.
7.55   Put soufflé in oven. Prepare starter.
8.00   Serve avocado with raspberry dressing.
8.10   Put water on to boil for vegetables.
8.15   Put vegetables on to cook.
8.25   (Or when soufflé is ready.) Serve main course.

Follow with walnut and honey tart served with cream.

Select your menu from these suggestions

Starters
Avocado soup

Watercress soup
Chilled prawn soup

Avocado with
raspberry dressing
Seafood mousse

Pâté

Roasted Stilton and
salad
Avocado and prawn
bake

Main courses
Salmon with
watercress sauce
Trout en croûte
Fish with prawn sauce

Stilton stuffed chicken
breasts
Individual beef
Wellingtons
Pork and apple strudel

Pigeon breasts in
wine sauce
Venison in cream
sauce
Bittersweet duck
breast
Classic cheese soufflé
Leek and Stilton bakes

Desserts
Walnut and honey tarts

Chocolate marquise
Crème caramel and
berries
Strawberry mousse
meringues
Whisky and walnut
parfait
Chocolate mousse
cases
Brandy brulée

Ginger syllabub

Starters

Avocado soup
Serves 4

    1oz (25g) butter
    1oz (25g) plain flour
    5floz (125ml) milk
    2 ripe avocados, peeled and stones removed
    25floz (625ml) vegetable or chicken stock
    white pepper
    Serve with:
    cream swirled into soup

Melt butter in saucepan. Take from the heat and beat in flour and a little of the milk; when smooth return to heat. Gradually stir in rest of milk until you have a very thick white sauce. Liquidize the avocado with a little of the stock and then blend all ingredients together. Return to the heat and heat soup gently until heated through. Serve with a garnish of cream.

Watercress soup
Serves 4

    1oz (25g) butter
    1 onion, chopped
    2 bunches watercress, washed
    1 pint (500ml) vegetable or chicken stock
    10floz (250ml) milk
    1 tablespoon (15ml) instant potato powder

Melt the butter in a saucepan and cook the onion until soft. Reserve some of the watercress to garnish the soup, add the rest of the watercress with the stock to the pan and bring to the boil. Simmer for 5 minutes. Liquidize or purée the contents of the pan before returning to the heat. Now blend the potato powder with a little of the milk and add this mixture with the remainder of the milk to the soup. Stir continuously while bringing to the boil, then simmer for a few minutes until soup is heated through. Serve the soup garnished with the reserved watercress.

Chilled prawn soup
Serves 4

    8oz (200g) unpeeled prawns
    1 pint (500ml) fish stock
    5floz (125ml) dry white wine
    1oz (25g) butter
    1oz (25g) plain flour
    1 teaspoon (5ml) tomato purée
    salt and pepper
    5floz (125ml) single cream

Peel the prawns and put the shells in a saucepan with the fish stock. Cover and simmer for 30 minutes. Sieve the stock and mix the stock with the white wine. Melt the butter and then remove from the heat and beat in the flour and a little of the stock mixture. Return to the heat and gradually add the rest of the mixture and tomato purée. Add two thirds of the shelled prawns and season with salt and pepper and simmer for 5 minutes. Liquidize and then leave to chill for at least 3 hours. Before serving add the cream and mix thoroughly. Serve garnished with the remaining prawns.

Seafood mousse
Serves 4

    4 whole large slices smoked salmon
    15floz (375ml) fish stock
    5floz (125ml) dry white wine
    12oz (300g) shelled prawns
    3oz (75g) butter
    4floz (100ml) double cream, whipped
    1 teaspoon (5ml) tomato purée
    Serve with:
    hot toast fingers

Carefully line 4 ramekins with the slices of smoked salmon. Boil the stock and wine together until you are left with only 2 tablespoons of thick liquid. Chill. Purée the reduced stock with the prawns and butter. Mix with the cream and tomato purée. Put into the salmon-lined ramekins and fold the edges over to cover as much of the mousse as possible. Refrigerate overnight. The mousses should be turned out on to small plates just before serving and be accompanied by hot fingers of toast.

Roasted Stilton and salad
Serves 4

>4 slices fresh French bread
>4oz (100g) Stilton cheese
>assorted salad leaves (i.e. lollo rosso, maché, little gem)
>*Serve with:*
>port-flavoured dressing (made as for French dressing (page
>   167) but substituting walnut oil for olive oil and port for
>   wine vinegar)

Slice the Stilton into 4. Put 1 slice on each piece of bread. Grill or bake in a hot oven until Stilton has melted. While waiting for Stilton to melt arrange some lettuce leaves on 4 small plates. Dress with salad dressing. When Stilton has melted put a slice of the Stilton covered bread in the middle of each plate. Serve immediately.

Pâté
Serves 4

>12oz (300g) chicken livers
>3oz (75g) butter
>1 onion, chopped
>1 clove garlic, crushed or chopped
>1 tablespoon (5ml) double cream
>1 tablespoon (15ml) brandy
>2 teaspoons (10ml) tomato purée
>melted butter
>sprinkling of paprika
>*Serve with:*
>hot toast fingers

Fry the chicken livers in half the butter until they change colour, add the onion and garlic and fry for 5 minutes. Remove from heat and cool. Purée in a blender with the cream, brandy and tomato purée. Then mix thoroughly with the remaining butter. Divide between 4 ramekins. Smooth the tops. Pour a small amount of melted butter over each. Sprinkle with paprika and leave to chill overnight. Serve with fingers of hot toast.

Avocado with raspberry dressing
Serves 4

    1 punnet fresh raspberries
    5floz (125ml) German white wine
    2 avocados

Purée the raspberries, then sieve to remove pips. Blend with the wine and divide the dressing between 4 small plates. Peel and de-stone the avocados. Slice each half and arrange on top of the sauce so that the sauce can be seen between the slices. Serve immediately.

Avocado and prawn bake
Serves 4   *Pre-heat oven to 200°C/400°F/Gas 6*

    1oz (25g) butter
    1oz (25g) flour
    5floz (125ml) milk
    2oz (50g) Gruyère, grated
    2 ripe avocados
    1 clove garlic, chopped or crushed
    2oz (50g) cooked shelled prawns
    4 dessertspoons (40ml) double cream
    4 dessertspoons (40ml) wholemeal breadcrumbs

Melt the butter, then remove from heat and beat in the flour and a little of the milk. Return to the heat and gradually stir in the remaining milk. Slowly bring to boil and let mixture thicken. Again remove from the heat and add the cheese. Peel, de-stone and mash the avocados and blend with the sauce. Add the garlic and prawns and then divide between 4 ramekins or pile back into avocado skins. Put 1 dessertspoon of cream on top of each mixture and then sprinkle with breadcrumbs. Bake in the pre-heated oven for 20 minutes or until breadcrumbs are brown and the mixture is sizzling.

Main courses

Salmon with watercress sauce

Serves 4   *Pre-heat oven to 180°C/350°F/Gas 4*

    4 salmon steaks
    melted butter
    lemon juice
    small bunch watercress, washed
    4 tablespoons (60ml) chopped fresh parsley
    sprinkling of dried dill
    5floz (125ml) soured cream
    salt and pepper
Serve with:
    new potatoes
    green vegetable

I find that fish is always nicer if cooked in the microwave, so if you do own one of these objects cover the salmon steaks with melted butter and a squeeze of lemon juice and cook for approximately 8 minutes or as directed by the manufacturers of your microwave. If however you do not own a microwave this is what you do.

Take 4 pieces of foil and on each place a salmon steak. Cover with melted butter and a squeeze of lemon and wrap the foil so that there is room around the steak but so that the parcel is completely sealed. Bake in the pre-heated oven for 20-25 minutes depending on the size of your steaks.

To make the sauce: liquidize all other ingredients. Season to taste. Arrange the sauce on 4 plates and when the salmon is cooked lay a salmon steak on each plate. Serve with new potatoes. Other suggested vegetables to go with this dish are mange-tout, broccoli or asparagus. This is really a sumptuous dish which heralds the arrival of spring and all its goodies.

Fish with prawn sauce
Serves 4   *Pre-heat oven to 180°C/350°F/Gas 4*

4 fillets white fish (e.g. cod)
melted butter
squeeze of lemon
sprinkling of dried dill
5floz (125ml) fish stock
5floz (125ml) dry white wine
2 teaspoons (10ml) tomato purée
5floz (125ml) double cream
8oz (200g) cooked shelled prawns
salt and pepper
Serve with:
new potatoes
courgettes

Take 4 pieces of foil and on each place a fillet of fish. Cover with melted butter and a squeeze of lemon juice. Sprinkle with dill. Wrap foil around fish so as to seal completely. Bake in the pre-heated oven for 20-25 minutes depending on the size of your fillets.

To make the sauce liquidize the stock, wine, tomato purée and cream with half the prawns. Season to taste, add the rest of the prawns and heat through gently. Arrange the sauce on 4 plates and when the fillets are cooked place 1 on each plate. Serve with new potatoes and courgettes.

Trout en croûte
Serves 4 *Pre-heat oven to 200°C/400°F/Gas 6*

If you want a dish that is incredibly easy to cook but splendidly impressive this is the one for you. Unfortunately you must have access to a friendly fishmonger unless you are confident that you can prepare the fish yourself.

> 2 trout, skinned and filleted
> 4oz (100g) fish or seafood pâté
> 4oz (100g) cooked seasoned rice
> 2 sheets ready-made filo pastry
> melted butter
> poppy seeds
> *Serve with:*
> new potatoes
> green salad

Trim the trout fillets into even rectangles, then divide the pâté into 4 portions and spread over the fillets. Do the same with the rice and finally top with the trout trimmings. Cut each sheet of filo into 2. Brush with melted butter. Place a fillet in the middle of the bottom half of a filo sheet. Roll the bottom of the filo up over the fillet and again brush with butter. Fold in the sides and again brush with butter. Then roll up the fillet from the bottom to enclose completely. Put on a baking tray, join underneath, brush with more melted butter and sprinkle with poppy seeds. Repeat with the other 3 fillets. Bake in the pre-heated oven for 20-25 minutes until brown and crisp. Serve immediately. Delicious!

Stilton stuffed chicken breasts
Serves 4

> 4 large breasts of chicken, skinned and boned
> 2oz (50g) Stilton
> 4oz (100g) butter
> 1 egg
> seasoned flour
> rolled oats
> oil for frying
> *Serve with:*
> melted redcurrant jelly with added port
> green vegetable
> new potatoes

Each chicken breast should have a smaller fillet attached to it which was the top of the wing. Remove the smaller fillet from each breast and then flatten both the breast and fillet. Crumble the Stilton and mix with half the butter and then divide this mixture into 4. Roll each into a small cylinder, and wrap with 1 of the small fillets. Then wrap this with a chicken breast, so that the butter is fully enclosed. Beat the egg, then coat each breast with egg followed with seasoned flour and finally roll in the oats. Chill until firm. Fry in the remaining butter and a little oil until golden brown. Serve with melted redcurrant jelly or a fruity sauce to which port has been added, a green vegetable and new potatoes. The chicken can be kept warm in a cool oven for a short while if you do not wish to serve immediately.

Individual beef Wellingtons

Serves 4   *Pre-heat oven to 220°C/425°F/Gas 7*

4 fillet steaks
1 clove garlic, crushed or chopped
2oz (50g) butter
4oz (100g) firm meat pâté
4 sheets ready-rolled puff pastry
beaten egg to glaze
5floz (125ml) red wine
4oz (100g) mushrooms, thinly sliced
4 tablespoons (60ml) double cream
Serve with:
broccoli
baby carrots

Fry the steaks with the garlic in the butter very quickly just to seal the meat. Dry with kitchen towel and place a steak on each pastry sheet. Divide the pâté into 4 and place a slice on top of each steak. Roll out the pastry, if necessary, to a size large enough to enclose steak and pâté. Fold the pastry over the steak and pâté to make a small parcel. Trim and discard any spare pastry. Seal edges and make a small slit on the top of each parcel. Glaze with the beaten egg and chill for at least 30 minutes. Bake in the pre-heated oven on the top shelf for 13-18 minutes until pastry is browned and crisp. To make a gravy for the Wellingtons, pour the wine into the same pan that you used to seal the meat and heat quickly; add the mushrooms and cook for 1 minute. Add the cream and continue cooking while gravy reduces. Serve the beef Wellingtons with the sauce, broccoli and baby carrots.

Lamb noisettes
Serves 4

> 8 noisettes of lamb
> 4oz (100g) butter
> 5floz (125ml) red wine
> 1 large onion, thinly sliced
> 5floz (125ml) strong meat stock
> 1 teaspoon (5ml) cornflour
> 1 tablespoon (15ml) redcurrant jelly
> *Serve with:*
> tagliatelle
> button mushrooms

Quickly fry the lamb noisettes in butter over a fairly high heat. This should only take about 10 minutes. Remove to a casserole dish and slurp a little of the wine over the noisettes. Put in a cool oven to keep warm. In the same pan now fry the onions. When brown, add the rest of the wine and the stock. Simmer quickly. Mix the cornflour with a little water and add to the pan. Stir until sauce thickens. Add the redcurrant jelly and continue stirring until the jelly has melted into the sauce. Pour this sauce over the noisettes and leave in the oven for 20 minutes at least to let the flavours mingle. Serve with tagliatelle and button mushrooms.

Pork and apple strudel
Serves 4   *Pre-heat oven to 200°C/400°F/Gas 6*

> 16oz (400g) pork fillet
> 1 apple, peeled and cored
> 1 onion, chopped
> 2oz (50g) butter
> 4oz (100g) cream cheese
> pinch of dried sage
> 2 sheets filo pastry
> melted butter
> sesame seeds
> 1 teaspoon (5ml) wholegrain mustard
> 1 tablespoon (15ml) brandy
> 5floz (125ml) double cream
> *Serve with:*
> new potatoes
> peas

Cut both the pork and apple into small cubes. Fry with the onion in the butter until beginning to brown. Strain from the pan, leaving the juices, and mix with the cheese and sage. Brush each sheet of filo pastry with melted butter and cut in half. Divide the pork mixture into 4 portions. Place 1 portion on each pastry sheet, putting it in the middle of the bottom half of the pastry. Bring the bottom of the pastry up over the pork to cover it. Brush with butter and fold outside edges in over the pork. Brush with butter again and then roll the pastry up from the bottom. Place on a baking tray and brush with butter once more before sprinkling with sesame seeds. Bake in the pre-heated oven for 20 minutes until pastry is crisp and golden. To make a sauce to serve with the strudels, add the mustard and brandy to the pan juices and heat quickly. Add the cream and continue cooking until the sauce reduces.

Pigeon breasts in wine sauce
Serves 4
Don't be put off this dish if you can only obtain whole frozen pigeons rather than pigeon breasts. Once defrosted it is extremely quick and easy to remove the breasts. Just remember to cut down from the breastbones.

8 pigeon breasts
4oz (100g) butter
5floz (125ml) red wine
5floz (125ml) strong meat stock
1 teaspoon (5ml) cornflour
1 tablespoon (15ml) cranberry and port sauce
Serve with:
new potatoes
raisined cabbage (page 163)

Quickly fry the pigeon breasts in the butter. Remove to a casserole dish. Slurp a little of the wine over them and put in a cool oven to keep warm. Add the rest of the wine and the stock to the pan and heat briskly. Mix the cornflour with some water to make a smooth paste and add this also to the pan. Stir while sauce thickens. Lastly add the cranberry sauce and heat through. Pour this sauce over the breasts and leave for at least 20 minutes in a cool oven. Serve with new potatoes and raisined cabbage.

Venison in cream sauce

Serves 4

    20oz (500g) loin of venison,
        sliced into thin strips
    1 tablespoon redcurrant jelly
    3 tablespoons (45ml) red wine
    seasoned flour
    3oz (75g) butter
    1 large onion, thinly sliced
    8oz (200g) mushrooms, thinly sliced
    10floz (250ml) soured cream
    salt and pepper
    Serve with:
    rice
    green vegetable

Marinate the venison in the jelly and wine overnight. To cook, drain venison strips from marinade, coat with the flour and fry quickly in the butter. Remove the meat from the pan, add the onion and cook until brown. Add the mushrooms and again fry quickly. Return the meat to the pan and add the soured cream. Heat through and season to taste before serving on a bed of rice with a green vegetable.

Bittersweet duck breast

Serves 4

    4 duck breasts, boned
    1oz (25g) butter
    1 Seville orange, grated rind and juice
    1 lemon, grated rind and juice
    1 tablespoon (15ml) sugar
    1 tablespoon (15ml) brandy
    1 tablespoon (15ml) cornflour
    Serve with:
    sauté potatoes
    raisined cabbage (page 163)

Grill the duck breasts under a medium grill for 6-7 minutes, turning once. While cooking the duck put all other ingredients apart from cornflour in a saucepan. Bring to boil and then simmer for 4 minutes. Blend cornflour with a little water to make a smooth paste and add to sauce. Stir as sauce thickens. When duck is cooked serve with sauce poured over the duck breasts with sauté potatoes and raisined cabbage.

Classic cheese soufflé
Serves 4   *Pre-heat oven to 190°C/375°F/Gas 5*

2oz (50g) butter
1oz (25g) plain flour
½oz (15g) cornflour
10floz (250ml) milk
3oz (75g) Gruyère cheese, grated
1 tablespoon (15ml) Parmesan cheese, grated
4 eggs, separated
½ teaspoon (3ml) wholegrain mustard
salt and pepper
Serve with:
new potatoes
green vegetable or salad

Melt butter in a saucepan, remove from heat and add flour, corn-flour and a little milk. Return to heat and gradually add the rest of the milk, stirring continuously. Add the cheeses and beat in the egg yolks one by one. Season with the mustard and salt and pepper. Whisk the egg whites until stiff. Carefully but thoroughly fold in a quarter of the whites, then gently fold in the rest. Put in a buttered soufflé dish measuring 6 inches/15cm or holding 2 pints/1.2 litres. Bake in the pre-heated oven for 30-40 minutes. DO NOT OPEN THE OVEN DOOR FOR THE FIRST 30 MINUTES. The soufflé is cooked when it is well-risen and brown and does not wobble when the dish is slightly shaken. IT MUST BE SERVED IMMEDIATELY, so make sure the new potatoes and green vegetable or salad are already on the table.

Leek and Stilton bakes

Serves 4   *Pre-heat oven to 200°C/400°F/Gas 6*

    12oz (300g) leeks, finely sliced
    2 cloves garlic, crushed or chopped
    2oz (50g) butter
    4 eggs, beaten
    2oz (50g) fresh breadcrumbs
    4oz (100g) Stilton, grated
    sprinkling of ground mace
    Serve with:
    melted redcurrant jelly with added port
    green vegetable
    new potatoes

Gently fry the leeks and garlic in the butter until soft. Remove from heat and add all other ingredients and mix well. Thoroughly butter 4 ramekins and divide the mixture between them. Smooth the tops and glaze with melted redcurrant jelly. Bake in the pre-heated oven for 15-25 minutes. Stand ramekins on a wet tea towel for 1 minute, then run a knife around the edges of the ramekins to turn out, so that glazed side is uppermost. Serve with extra melted redcurrant jelly if wished and a green vegetable and new potatoes.

Desserts

Walnut and honey tarts
Serves 4

Pre-heat oven to 200°C/400°F/Gas 6

  8oz (200g) shortcrust pastry
  3oz (75g) unsalted butter
  5oz (125g) soft brown sugar
  3 eggs, beaten
  4 tablespoons (60ml) clear honey
  few drops vanilla essence
  4oz (100g) walnut halves
  Serve with:
  single cream

Roll out the pastry and cut 4 rounds large enough to line the indentations of a 4-hole Yorkshire pudding tray. Grease the moulds and line with pastry. Put a round of greaseproof paper in each and weight down with some coins. Bake in the pre-heated oven for 6 minutes. Allow to cool before removing the hot coins! This is known as 'baking blind'. Blend the butter and sugar until creamy. Then slowly beat in the eggs. Finally add the honey and vanilla essence. Blend well. Reserve 4 walnut halves and sprinkle the rest in the bottom of the pastry cases (have you removed the greaseproof paper?), then divide the honey mixture between the pastry cases. Bake again for 35-45 minutes until the pastry is brown and the filling is set. Garnish each pastry with a reserved walnut half and leave to cool. Serve cold in a pool of cream.

Whisky and walnut parfait
Serves 4

  4 egg yolks
  3oz (75g) soft brown sugar
  5floz (125ml) double cream, lightly whipped
  2 tablespoons (30ml) whisky
  2oz (50g) shelled walnuts, chopped
  4 walnut halves

Whisk the egg yolks in a bowl over a pan of boiling water until they are creamy and smooth and have increased in bulk. Remove from heat and slowly whisk in the sugar. (If this is done with an electric mixer it will increase the bulk considerably, but do not overwhisk.) Fold in the cream, whisky and chopped nuts. Put into ramekins and freeze overnight. Put into fridge to soften 1 hour before serving and decorate each ramekin with a walnut half.

Crème caramel and berries

Serves 4 *Pre-heat oven to 160°C/325°F/Gas 3*

Caramel:
8 tablespoons (120ml) caster sugar
4 tablespoons water
Crème:
12floz (300ml) milk
4 tablespoons (60ml) double cream
2oz (50g) sugar
few drops vanilla essence
2 eggs plus 1 egg yolk
8oz (200g) mixed berries (e.g. raspberries and redcurrants)

Put sugar and water for caramel in a saucepan and bring to boil, cook quickly until mixture turns golden brown and syrupy and remove from heat immediately. DO NOT OVERCOOK. Divide between 4 ramekins. To make the crème put the milk, cream, sugar and vanilla essence into a milk pan and heat through. Do not boil. Turn heat off and leave for 5 minutes. Beat eggs and egg yolk until, thick and creamy. Slowly beat milk into eggs. Using a muslin cloth in a sieve, strain the mixture into the ramekins. Place the ramekins in a roasting tin and pour enough boiling water into the pan to come halfway up the ramekins. Be careful not to splash any water into the ramekins themselves. Bake in the pre-heated oven for 30-35 minutes until the centres are firm when pressed lightly. Remove from tin and leave to cool: chill in refrigerator for at least 2 hours. To serve, run a knife around the edges of the ramekins and invert onto a small plate. The caramel syrup should be poured over the crème. Decorate each plate with some of the berries and serve immediately.

Chocolate marquise

Serves 4

> 6oz (150g) dark plain chocolate
> 4 tablespoons (60ml) brandy
> 6oz (150g) unsalted butter
> 6oz (150g) caster sugar
> 4 egg yolks
> 6floz (150ml) whipping cream, lightly whipped
> *Serve with:*
> puréed raspberries

Melt the chocolate (either in a bowl over hot water or in the microwave) and add the brandy. Beat the butter and half the sugar until creamy. Beat the egg yolks with the remaining sugar. Beat the butter and sugar mixture into the chocolate, then stir in the egg mixture. Finally fold in the whipped cream. Line 4 ramekins with clingfilm, and fill with mixture. Chill overnight. Serve from fridge. Take out of clingfilm and invert on to small plates; serve with a purée of raspberries.

Chocolate mousse cases

Serves 4

> 6oz (150g) dark plain chocolate
> 4 eggs, separated
> 1 tablespoon (15ml) Tia Maria
> *Serve with:*
> single cream

Melt the chocolate in a bowl over hot water (or in the microwave). Using a pastry brush, paint the inside of 8 paper baking cases with some of the chocolate. Try to get an even coating which completely covers the inside. Leave to harden. Whisk the egg whites and beat the egg yolks. Beat the yolks into the remaining chocolate and then add the Tia Maria. Fold in the whisked egg whites. Divide the mousse mixture between the chocolate cases. Chill in the refrigerator until set. Before serving gently peel off the paper cases. Serve in a pool of cream.

Brandy brulée

Serves 4   *Pre-heat oven to 160°C/325°F/Gas 3*

    4 egg yolks, well beaten
    1½oz (40g) caster sugar
    16floz (400ml) double cream
    4 tablespoons (60ml) brandy
    additional caster sugar for topping

Mix together all ingredients except additional sugar and divide between 4 ramekins. Place in a roasting tin and pour in enough boiling water to come halfway up the ramekins. (Be careful not to splash any water into the ramekins.) Now bake in the pre-heated oven for 30 minutes. Remove from tin and leave to cool. Chill overnight. About 2 hours before you are to serve the brulée, cover the top of each crème with a layer of caster sugar. THE TOP OF THE CRÈME MUST BE FULLY COVERED WITH SUGAR. Pre-heat a grill to its hottest temperature. Put the crèmes under the grill and watch carefully. As soon as the sugar has melted, remove. Chill until the caramel top is crisp. To eat: break through the caramel topping and eat the creamy custard with the crisp topping. Absolutely delicious.

Strawberry mousse meringues

Serves 4

    4 egg yolks
    4oz (100g) caster sugar
    5floz (125ml) sieved strawberries
    ½oz (15g) powdered gelatine
    5floz (125ml) whipping cream, lightly whipped
    4 ready-made meringue cases
    Serve with:
    a few whole strawberries

Whisk the egg yolks with the sugar and fold in the strawberry purée. Dissolve the gelatine in 3 tablespoons (45ml) water according to the manufacturer's directions. Stir this into the strawberry mixture. Fold in the whipped cream. Pile this mixture into the meringue cases and leave to set. Serve decorated with the whole strawberries.

Ginger syllabub

Serves 4

    10floz (250ml) double cream
    2 tablespoons (30ml) ginger marmalade
    2 tablespoons (30ml) brandy
    Serve with:
    brandy snaps

Whip the cream stiffly, then fold in the ginger marmalade and the brandy. Pile into long-stemmed glasses and chill for at least 1 hour. Serve with brandy snaps to dip into the syllabub.

5. Guests to stay

It is always pleasant when friends or family come to stay for a few days. Usually this is over a holiday period or the weekend. As their stay is so short I feel it is nice to push the boat out a little for them. Everyone likes to be pampered, and with just a little effort on your part you can increase their enjoyment at staying with you tenfold. It is definitely the little things that count. DO make sure you have a cleaning blitz just before they arrive. No one enjoys staying in a house that is dirty. It is very easy to let the housework slide: in our day-to-day life we are often too busy to tackle all those chores about the house. However if guests are coming, look around the house with a fresh eye. You will obviously have cleared out the spare bedroom (if this is a luxury that you have), cleaned the bathroom and tidied and

95

vacuumed the sitting room. On a second look you may find that the paintwork has been collecting dirty fingerprints, the kitchen cupboards could all do with a wipe-down and the windows are filthy! These are all the sorts of jobs that we never quite get round to, so get out your cleaning cloth and take a good look round; you will be surprised at where the dirt collects!

Once you have sorted out where your guests will be sleeping and have found clean sheets or aired the sleeping bags, the next thing to do is to make some plans as to how you will spend your weekend, not forgetting that our weather is very variable! It's no use planning a picnic on a beach unless you have some idea of what to do if the heavens open just as you arrive. That's why I never make any elaborate plans when eating outside.

Picnics, in our terms, consist of plenty of cheeses, pâtés, fresh bread and fruit (which can also be used for an informal lunch at home if the weather turns nasty), sometimes some cooked chicken pieces or a good pork pie cut into wedges, and a rich fruit cake. Most people are happy with this sort of spread. Don't forget the drink! Some wine or beers, at least one bottle of soft drink and, if the weather is inclined to dither, a thermos of hot coffee.

Having made your plans you will know which meals you will be providing during the weekend and can pre-pare accordingly.

It is generally a good idea to cook a meal for your guests if they are arriving on Friday evening. When travelling is involved, people invariably arrive late and are not usually inclined to go straight out again. Of course you could provide a takeaway, but I'm sure you are able to produce something that is tastier! The humble casserole is a good choice for a Friday night meal; if your friends are late you can always turn the oven down and the food will not spoil. If you are entertaining your guests on Saturday night as well, prepare the starter and dessert for this meal before they arrive.

On the Sunday you will either be going out for the day (and eating lunch at a pub) or resting at home and preparing a Sunday roast. If you are out all day it is nice to give them a decent tea before they leave, whereas if you have had a blow-out lunch it is highly unlikely that people will even be capable of moving again before they have to depart for home!

So prepare in advance and both you and your guests will have a good time. One last word. If you have a family pet, do limit its access to your guests. Not everyone appreciates being woken at the crack of dawn by a wet nose!

Friday night

As your guests are travelling to stay with you, they will obviously not be arriving until some time in the evening. Make sure that you have prepared everything before they arrive so that you are free to spend all your time with them. If they have driven over to see you, they will probably be harassed and in need of a drink.

I always provide a few nuts and assorted crisps to nibble on (for us while we're waiting for them – and for them when they arrive). This means that you haven't got to rush off and finish the dinner the moment they arrive, starving, on your doorstep. The perfect starter to this meal is a dip (see page 132), as it can be fully prepared beforehand. Do not serve it in individual portions as you would for a posh dinner party. Travellers will be too tired, at the end of a hard day's work and then travelling, for anything posh. Make this a casual, very relaxed affair by placing the dip in the middle of the table and inviting people to help themselves. Next serve a casserole with jacket baked potatoes and a green vegetable. Follow with a good selection of cheeses that people can linger over, and you will have the perfect meal for friends. The following 3 casseroles are well-tested favourites of mine.

Normandy pheasant
Serves 4   *Pre-heat oven 180°C/350°F/Gas 4*
    1 oven-ready pheasant
    2oz (50g) unsalted butter
    2oz (50g) smoked bacon, chopped
    1 onion, chopped
    2 cloves garlic, crushed or chopped
    8oz (200g) cooking apples, cored and sliced
    10floz (150ml) dry cider
    1 dessertspoon (10ml) redcurrant jelly
    5floz (125ml) double cream
    chopped fresh parsley
Serve with:
    jacket baked potatoes
    broccoli

Fry the pheasant in half the butter until browned. Remove from pan to casserole dish. Next fry bacon, onion and garlic, add these to casserole dish. Finally add the rest of the butter and fry apples until tender. Gradually add cider and redcurrant jelly. Mix well and simmer for a few minutes, stirring. Pour sauce over pheasant. Cover and cook in the pre-heated oven for 1½ hours. Remove the pheasant from casserole and let cool a little while you liquidize the sauce. Blend with the cream. Next joint the pheasant, cutting the thighs and drumsticks from the bird and then cutting the bird in half along the breastbone and backbone. Rearrange the pheasant in the casserole dish and pour the sauce over it. Reduce the temperature of the oven, putting it on a cool setting, and return the casserole to the oven until you are ready for it. Sprinkle with parsley before serving with jacket baked potatoes and broccoli.

Beef carbonnade

Serves 4   *Pre-heat oven to 180°C/350°F/Gas 4*

2 onions, finely sliced
2 cloves garlic, crushed or chopped
1 tablespoon (15ml) oil
2lb (800g) lean braising beef, cubed
3 tablespoons (45ml) flour
sprinkling of paprika
2 teaspoons (10ml) brown sugar
1 tablespoon (15ml) wholegrain mustard
15floz (375ml) brown ale
2 tablespoons (30ml) strong beef stock
sprinkling of dried French herbs
8 slices French bread
Serve with:
jacket baked potatoes
green beans

Fry onion and garlic in oil until brown. Remove to a casserole dish. Coat meat with flour and paprika and fry until brown. Add sugar and mustard. Mix well and transfer to casserole dish. Mix ale, stock and herbs and pour over meat. Cook in the pre-heated oven for 2 hours. (If you prefer a thicker gravy add some cornflour blended with water 30 minutes before cooking time is finished.) Leave in a cool oven. When nearly ready to serve, put oven up to 200°C/400°F/Gas 6. Press each slice of bread into the meat juices and then turn over and lay on top of casserole. Finish by cooking uncovered for 15 minutes until bread topping is crisp. Serve with jacket baked potatoes and green beans.

Coq au vin

Serves 4   *Pre-heat oven to 180°C/350°F/Gas 4*

1 chicken, jointed and breasts cut into 4 pieces
2 large onions, thinly sliced or 16 small pickling onions
2 cloves garlic, crushed or chopped
sprinkling of dried French herbs
8oz (200g) mushrooms, quartered
1 bottle French red wine
4 tablespoons (60ml) flour
sprinkling of paprika
2 tablespoons (30ml) oil
2oz (50g) butter
2 tablespoons (30ml) tomato purée
14-oz (400-g) can chopped tomatoes
Serve with:
jacket baked potatoes
courgettes

Marinate the chicken, onions, garlic, herbs, and mushrooms in the wine overnight. Remove chicken pieces and dry, coat with flour and paprika mixed together. Cook in oil and butter in a frying pan until golden brown. Put in a casserole dish. Remove vegetables from marinade and dry well. Fry vegetables until brown in fat in pan; add to casserole. Add tomato purée and tomatoes to frying pan, together with the marinade mixture. Bring to boil and simmer for a few minutes. Pour over chicken and vegetables. Cook casserole in the pre-heated oven for 1½ hours until chicken is very tender. Keep in a cool oven until ready to serve with jacket baked potatoes and courgettes.

Saturday

Don't fall into the trap of preparing a cooked breakfast today: it will eat into the time you have to spend with your guests. Take this opportunity to show your friends some of your local attractions or organize a shopping expedition. If the weather is fine take some bread and cheeses and go for an impromptu picnic. If the weather is typically British, head for the pub. Do return at a reasonable hour so that everyone has a chance to sit down and relax before the evening. Make sure your guests feel free to take a bath and prepare themselves. It is nice to dress up, even if you are just eating at home.

I suggest a pre-prepared starter that you could make the day before and a cold dessert which can also be made in advance (see page 105). Don't forget that there is a wide range of dinner-party desserts for sale in the shops, which are impressive without being any bother for the host. If you are really going to town, prepare a few nibbles and add a cheese course to the menu. Both are easily done but will still only leave you with the main course to prepare on the night. The main course should be both simple and quick to prepare, leaving you cheerful and fit to entertain your guests.

Starters ─────────────────────────────────

Fish pâté
Serves 4
> 2 smoked mackerel fillets, skinned and flaked
> 6oz (150g) unsalted butter, softened
> 1 teaspoon (5ml) wholegrain mustard
> 1 tablespoon (15ml) sherry
> 1 tablespoon (15ml) lemon juice
> freshly ground pepper
> *Serve with:*
> fingers of hot toast

Blend all ingredients together in a liquidiser and pile into ramekin dishes. Cover with clingfilm and leave at least 24 hours before serving with fingers of hot toast.

Potted shrimps
Serves 4

   12oz (300g) cooked peeled shrimps
   8oz (200g) unsalted butter
   sprinkling of ground mace
   freshly ground black pepper
   Serve with:
   brown bread or hot toast triangles

Put the shrimps into a mixing bowl. Heat the butter until frothing, skim off the froth. Pour three quarters of the butter on to the prawns, add the mace and pepper and mix well. Put into 4 ramekins and cover with the remaining butter. Chill for 24 hours before serving with brown bread or hot toast triangles.

Cheese pâté
Serves 4

   4oz (100g) soft full fat cheese
   2oz (50g) unsalted butter, softened
   4oz (100g) Stilton or Cheshire cheese, grated
   4 tablespoons (60ml) double cream
   1 teaspoon (5ml) wholegrain mustard
   1 tablespoon (15ml) chopped chives
   Serve with:
   melba toast

Blend the cream cheese with the butter, add the Stilton or Cheshire and blend again. Add the cream, mustard and chives and mix well. Put into ramekins and cover with clingfilm. Chill overnight.

Main courses

Pan-fried lamb and apricots
Serves 4
- 4-8 lean lamb chops (depending on size)
- 4 small onions, quartered
- 2oz (50g) butter
- 1 teaspoon (5ml) curry powder
- 8-oz (200-g) can apricot halves in natural fruit juice

Serve with:
- rice
- green vegetable

Fry the chops and onions in the butter for 10 minutes, turning frequently. Add the curry powder and cook for another minute. Finally add the canned apricots and juice. Simmer until juice reduces slightly. Serve immediately.

Spiced nutty pork
Serves 4
- 3 tablespoons (45ml) crunchy peanut butter
- 1 tablespoon (15ml) muscovado sugar
- 1 tablespoon (15ml) dark soy sauce
- 1 teaspoon (5ml) sweet chilli sauce
- 4 pork chops

Serve with:
- fruit pilaff (see page 160)

Blend the peanut butter, sugar, soy sauce and chilli sauce together. Use to cover pork chops. Grill on a high heat until chops are cooked (about 5 minutes for each side); serve immediately with fruit pilaff.

Trout with almonds
Serves 4
2oz (50g) flaked almonds
2oz (50g) butter
4 rainbow trout, gutted
1 tablespoon (15ml) chopped chives
squeeze lemon juice
Serve with:
new or jacket baked potatoes
green vegetable

Fry almonds gently in half the butter until brown. Remove from pan and fry trout in rest of butter for 5 minutes each side. Add chives and lemon juice and continue to cook for a few minutes, until you are sure the trout is done (the fish will flake when prodded). Serve immediately with potatoes and a green vegetable.

Desserts

If you have time the day before make a cold dessert to keep in the refrigerator, such as Chocolate cheesecake (page 42), No-cook cake (page 45) or Strawberry tart (page 44).

If you did not have the time to make up a dessert serve one of the many gâteaux or frozen desserts that you can now buy in the shops. Only do remember to take it out of the freezer in time!

Sunday

I think whether or not you should cook a full British breakfast for your guests depends on your plans for the day. If you intend just to laze around reading the papers (my favourite way of spending Sunday morning) and then have a traditional roast lunch, a full cooked breakfast is unnecessary. If you are going out it is a good idea to start the day with a cooked breakfast. On the other hand if you are late risers you won't have time for a full breakfast before it's time to be off. A good compromise is lots of fruit juice and scrambled eggs with slices of a good ham, if you feel you must offer something cooked, otherwise croissants served with good coffee go down well. For really late risers fresh fruit such as grapefruit or melon is a good choice.

If you do go out, on your return it is nice to round off your weekend with Sunday tea. In summer, I would keep this very light; perhaps some scones and a slice of lemon cake (pages 112 and 111). Winter, however, calls for more of an effort. Hot muffins and crumpets, served with butter and jam, are very comforting, followed by some small cakes such as spiced rock cakes and a slice of rich fruit cake (pages 112 and 113). Gingerbread (page 125) is also a popular choice.

If you have stayed at home and had a Sunday lunch, an afternoon tea should not be necessary; however I find that a slice of fruit cake with a cup of tea is just the right note on which to end the weekend.

Sunday roasts

A roast lunch always goes down well. It is not necessary to prepare a starter to this meal, although occasionally we do put out some nuts to nibble on if we are indulging in a few gin-and-tonics before lunch. This is usually a blow-out affair and *should* sensibly be accompanied by a light dessert, but no! This is the time to make a REAL pudding, something that can be made up while preparing the meal and popped into the oven to cook as the main course is being consumed. However, do allow a rest period before going on to the pudding. I find at least 20 minutes is needed before people are ready to attempt the next course. Afterwards the only possible activity is putting your feet up and having a snooze!

Roast chicken
Allow approximately 12oz (300g) per person (i.e. 3lb (1.2kg) chicken will serve 4 people).

Brush with oil and sprinkle with salt and paprika. Place in a roasting tin with lard or oil. Roast in a pre-heated oven at 200°C/400°F/Gas 6 for 20 minutes per pound plus 20 minutes (i.e. 1 hour 20 minutes for a 3lb (1.2kg) chicken). Baste occasionally with juices from tin.

Serve with roast potatoes, sweetcorn, carrots and peas. Stuffing and a thin gravy are also usually served. In the summer, cold roast chicken is good with a green salad and new potatoes. In fact the ideal summer Sunday lunch.

Roast pork
Allow approximately 6oz (150g) per person when boned and rolled (i.e. 1½lb (600g) joint for 4 people).

Rub the rind with oil and salt to ensure a crisp crackling. Place in a roasting tin with some dripping or lard. Bake in a pre-heated oven at 200°C/400°F/Gas 6 for 30 minutes per lb plus 35 minutes (i.e. 1 hour 20 minutes for a 1½lb (600g) joint). Baste occasionally with the juices from the tin. Remove the crackling to carve the meat and serve separately.

Serve with roast potatoes and parsnips, cauliflower and peas. Stuffing, apple sauce or wholegrain mustard and thickened gravy are also served.

Roast lamb

Allow approximately 12oz (300g) per person (i.e. 3lb (1.2kg) joint for 4 people).

Sprinkle with some fresh herbs such as rosemary or thyme. Place in a roasting tin with some dripping or lard and bake in a pre-heated oven at 220°C/425°F/Gas 7 for 20 minutes per lb plus 20 minutes (i.e. 1 hour 20 minutes for a 3lb (1.2kg) joint). Baste occasionally with juices from the tin.

Serve with roast potatoes, peas and broccoli. Mint sauce or red-currant jelly and a thickened gravy are also served.

Roast beef

Allow approximately 8oz (200g) per person if meat is boned and rolled (i.e. 2lb (800g) boned and rolled joint for 4 people). Allow approximately 12oz (300g) per person if meat is on the bone (i.e. 3lb (1.2kg) joint for 4 people).

Place in roasting tin with beef dripping and bake in a pre-heated oven at 220°C/425°F/Gas 7 for 25 minutes per lb plus 25 minutes if boned and rolled (i.e. 1 hour 15 minutes for a 2lb (800g) boned and rolled joint). Bake for 20 minutes per lb plus 20 minutes if meat is on the bone (i.e. 1 hour 20 minutes for a 3lb (1.2kg) joint), basting occasionally with juices from tin. If you like your beef rare deduct 5 minutes per lb when calculating your cooking times.

Serve with roast potatoes, cauliflower cheese or broccoli, carrots and peas. Yorkshire pudding, mustard or horseradish sauce and a rich gravy should also be served.

Special roasting pans can be bought which are self basting. Or you can buy trivets which fit in your roasting pan and on which you place the meat. It is therefore not cooked in any fat and is healthier for you.

Puddings

Treacle tart

Serves 4-6   *Pre-heat oven to 200°C/400°F/Gas 6*

    4oz (100g) self-raising flour
    2oz (50g) butter
    5 tablespoons (75ml) golden syrup
    1 tablespoon (15ml) black treacle
    6 tablespoons (90ml) white breadcrumbs
    1 dessertspoon (10ml) orange juice
    grated rind 1 orange
    Serve with:
    whipped cream

Rub the butter into the flour and gradually work into a dough, using a little cold water if needed. Roll out to fit an 8-inch (20cm) flan tin. Warm the tins of syrup and treacle in a dish of hot water. Sprinkle the breadcrumbs, orange juice and grated rind into the flan dish. Using a warm spoon measure out the syrup and treacle and pour over the breadcrumbs. Do not mix in. Bake in the pre-heated oven for 25 minutes and let cool slightly before serving with whipped cream.

Rich bread-and-butter pudding

Serves 4-6   *Pre-heat oven to 220°C/425°F/Gas 7*

    2oz (50g) glacé cherries
    3 tablespoons (45ml) whisky or 2floz (50ml) orange juice
    4oz (100g) sultanas
    10 slices bread, buttered
    1oz (25g) brown sugar
    4 eggs, beaten
    1½ pints (900ml) milk

Chop the cherries and soak in the whisky or orange juice with the sultanas for 15 minutes. Cut the bread into triangles and use just over half to line a greased ovenproof dish. Sprinkle the fruit, sugar and whisky or juice on the bread. Place the remaining slices of bread on top. Beat the eggs and milk together and pour over the bread. Bake in the pre-heated oven for 45 minutes. Serve hot.

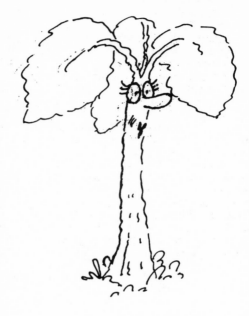

Rhubarb Charlotte

Serves 4-6   *Pre-heat oven to 200°C/400°F/Gas 6*

1lb (400g) rhubarb, trimmed and cut into small lengths
3oz (75g) unsalted butter
6oz (150g) wholemeal breadcrumbs
1 teaspoon (5ml) allspice
2oz (50g) brown sugar
2 tablespoons (30ml) orange juice
2 tablespoons (30ml) clear honey
Serve with:
lightly whipped cream

Fry the rhubarb gently in half the butter until soft. Remove from pan. Add the rest of the butter and breadcrumbs and stir until butter is absorbed. Layer the rhubarb and breadcrumbs into a buttered ovenproof dish, finishing with a layer of breadcrumbs. Mix rest of ingredients and pour over breadcrumbs. Bake in the pre-heated oven for 15-25 minutes or until top is brown. Serve with whipped cream.

Tarte tatin

Serves 4-6 *Pre-heat oven to 220°C/425°F/Gas 7*

8oz (200g) butter
2 egg yolks, beaten
2oz (50g) caster sugar
grated rind of ½ lemon
6oz (150g) plain flour
pinch salt
3lb (1.2kg) dessert apples, peeled, cored and sliced thickly
2oz (50g) muscovado sugar
Serve with:
whipped cream

Chop three quarters of the butter into very small pieces and then add egg yolks and caster sugar. Mix well. Add lemon rind and then sift in flour and salt. Mix in. You should now have a crumbly mixture. Knead into a dough and chill for 30 minutes. Fry apples in remaining butter and muscovado sugar for 10 minutes until brown and golden. Put in the bottom of a buttered loose-bottomed 8-inch (20cm) cake tin. Knead out dough to fit on top of the apples; the round should completely cover them. Press down lightly. Bake in the pre-heated oven for 15-20 minutes or until dough is risen and brown. Leave to cool slightly and then turn out on to a plate to serve with whipped cream.

Afternoon tea

Lemon cake

Makes 6-8 slices *Pre-heat oven to 180°C/350°F/Gas 4*

4oz (100g) butter
8oz (200g) caster sugar
2 eggs, beaten
4oz (100g) self-raising flour
1 lemon, rind and juice

Beat the butter with half the sugar until creamy. Beat in the eggs and then mix in the flour. Stir in the lemon rind. Put in a greased loose-bottomed 8-inch (20cm) cake tin and bake in the pre-heated oven for 40 minutes or until cake has set and feels firm to the touch. Turn the cake out on to a wire rack. Mix the remaining sugar with the lemon juice and spoon carefully over the cake. Leave to cool and a sugar crust will form on the cake.

Scones

Makes 8   *Pre-heat oven to 220°C/425°F/Gas 7*

> 8oz (200g) self-raising flour
> pinch of salt
> 2 teaspoons (10ml) baking powder
> 2oz (50g) butter
> 1 egg, beaten
> 2 tablespoons (30ml) milk
> *Serve with:*
> jam
> whipped cream

Sieve the flour, salt and baking powder together and then, using fingers, rub the butter into the flour. Mix the egg and milk together and mix enough into the flour mixture to make a soft dough. Press the dough out into a round just under 1 inch (2cm) thick. Cut out small circles. Put on a greased baking tray. Brush tops with any left-over egg mixture (or plain milk) to glaze. Bake in the pre-heated oven for 10-15 minutes until browned and risen. Serve with jam and whipped cream.

Spiced rock cakes

Makes 8   *Pre-heat oven to 200°C/400°F/Gas 6*

> 8oz (200g) self-raising wholemeal flour
> 1 teaspoon (5ml) allspice
> 1 teaspoon (5ml) ginger
> 4oz (100g) butter
> 3 tablespoons (45ml) demerara sugar
> 4oz (100g) mixed dried fruit
> 1 egg, beaten
> 1 tablespoon (15ml) milk

Mix the flour and spices together and then with fingers rub in the butter. Add two thirds of the sugar and rest of ingredients. Mix well. Put in little heaps on a greased baking tray (leaving a space around each as they spread), sprinkle with the rest of the sugar and bake in the pre-heated oven for 15 minutes until golden brown.

Rich fruit cake
Makes 8 slices

  12oz (300g) wholewheat flour
  2 teaspoons (10ml) allspice
  1 teaspoon (5ml) baking powder
  6oz (150g) good soft margarine
  6oz (150g) muscovado sugar
  8oz (200g) mixed·fruit, chopped
  4oz (100g) glacé cherries, quartered
  3 eggs, beaten
  3 tablespoons (45ml) milk

Grease and line the base of an 8-inch (20cm) loose-bottomed cake tin with greaseproof paper.

Sieve the flour, spice and baking powder into a bowl (add contents of sieve). Add all other ingredients and mix well. (If using an electric mixer, do not overbeat.) Put into the prepared tin and bake at 150°C/300°F/Gas 2 for 2-2½ hours. The cake is done when a skewer inserted into the middle comes out clean. Leave in tin for 10 minutes and then turn out and leave to cool on a wire rack. Make 1 week before you are going to eat it.

NOT VENISON AGAIN !

6. Christmas cooking

Christmas is the one time when you can't avoid the in-laws! Seriously, Christmas is a family time and can be a great deal of fun if properly prepared for. Please, please don't just invite family and then leave them to their own devices. Treat them as you would any other guests – familiarity doesn't have to breed contempt!

People often just think about Christmas dinner when inviting family. This is fine if your family are only coming for dinner, but as more and more families are separated by large distances your family is quite likely to be staying a few days. So think of this occasion as you would if it was a matter of entertaining guests for the weekend. Let's hope they will appreciate everything you do for them and reciprocate next year!

I really love Christmas. It is the culinary highlight of my year. But I do believe that the more work you put in beforehand the better the time will be when it comes.

Some people are only happy if all of their Christmas goodies are home-made. That is okay for them but I think it is foolish to try to do too much if you have a full-time job, whether it is at work or in the home. I personally make only a few mince pies (see below). You can buy good quality mincemeat for these in the shops – though the addition of another dash of brandy never hurts. The same goes for Christmas puddings and cakes. Not only can you get very good shop-bought ones, but they can be very expensive to make at home. They also have to be made well in advance as they need time to let their flavours develop.

Mince pies
Makes 18   *Pre-heat oven to 200°C/400°F/Gas 6*

These are my one concession to Christmas cooking. Although you can buy good mince pies in the shops, the almond in these makes them especially nice and well worth making.

  10oz (250g) plain flour
  1oz (25g) ground almonds
  6oz (150g) unsalted butter
  2oz (50g) icing sugar, sifted
  sprinkling of grated orange rind
  1 egg yolk, beaten
  3 tablespoons (45ml) milk
  9oz (225g) luxury mincemeat
  milk to glaze
  sprinkling of caster sugar
  Serve with:
  brandy butter

With fingers, rub butter into flour and almonds so that you have a crumb mixture. Add the sugar and orange rind, mix. Beat the egg yolk and milk together and add enough of this mixture to make a soft dough. Chill for 30 minutes. Roll out and cut 18 rounds from pastry using a pastry cutter. Put into greased bun tins. Put a teaspoon of mincemeat in each pastry case. From remaining pastry cut 18 tops for the pies. Moisten the edges of each and press on to pies. Make a small slit in the top of each and glaze with milk. Sprinkle with caster sugar and bake in the pre-heated oven for 15-20 minutes until brown.

Christmas Eve
Lunch_____

Your family will often arrive at lunchtime after their morning journey. After a welcoming drink (which, depending on your family, will be either a cup of tea or something stronger!), it is nice to sit down to something warm. A piping hot bowl of soup is ideal. Serve with warmed rolls or wedges of crusty brown bread.

If you then put out a cheeseboard and a selection of fruit and nuts, this will suit everybody, as those with a large appetite can keep eating until they are full, while those with a small appetite will probably only have a piece of fruit.

Chestnut soup
Serves 4-6

        8oz (200g) chestnuts or small tin chestnut purée
        2 large onions, sliced
        2 tablespoons (30ml) olive oil
        35floz (1 litre) chicken stock
        freshly ground black pepper
        Serve with:
        brown bread or rolls

If using fresh chestnuts, boil for 15 minutes and then peel. (Warning, they will be hot and peeling takes ages.) Fry the onion in the oil until soft. Add chestnuts or chestnut purée. Bring to the boil then cover and simmer for 45 minutes. Liquidize. Return to pan and reheat, season with black pepper and serve immediately with bread or rolls. Delicious and seasonal!

Buffet supper

The last thing you want to be doing on Christmas Eve is cooking! I prefer to lay on a buffet spread so that people can just help themselves when they feel hungry. Leave all the cooking until tomorrow!

Before the family arrives I cook a large glazed ham joint which I use as the centrepiece for this buffet spread, and I serve some jacket baked potatoes (page 158) with a selection of salads (page 166). I also make sure that I have nibbly things on the table and again the cheeseboard comes out. To finish we have an alcoholic fruit salad and a selection of chocolates. I bake a *large* ham as it is very useful cold. I serve it with scrambled eggs for breakfast and bring it out with the other cold meats on Boxing Day.

Glazed ham

When you are working out how big a ham you will need, allow about 5-6oz (125-150g) meat per serving.

ham joint   *Pre-heat oven to 180°C/350°F/Gas 4*
5floz (125ml) apple juice
oil for roasting
cloves
4 tablespoons (60ml) fine-cut marmalade
4 tablespoons (60ml) clear honey
sprinkling of paprika
Serve with:
Cumberland sauce

Put the ham in a large saucepan with the apple juice; add enough water to cover. Bring to boil and draw off the scum that will form on the water. Cover and simmer. To calculate the cooking time allow 20 minutes per lb plus 20 minutes. (For small ham joints under 6lbs allow 25 minutes per lb.) Simmer for half of the cooking time. Drain and remove the rind from the ham. Score the fat into diamonds and stud with cloves. Roast in the pre-heated oven until 40 minutes before cooking time is up. Mix the marmalade, honey and paprika. Glaze the ham with a third of this mixture, return the ham to oven and roast for 10 minutes, glaze with another third of mixture. Repeat this, roasting the final time for 20 minutes. Remove from oven and leave to go cold. Serve thinly sliced with Cumberland sauce.

Cumberland sauce
Serves 8

    2 oranges, rind and juice
    2 lemons, rind and juice
    5floz (125ml) redcurrant jelly
    5floz (125ml) port or red wine
    2 dessertspoons (20ml) arrowroot

Very thinly pare the rinds from the oranges and lemons. Cut into very narrow strips. Put the rinds in a small saucepan, cover with water and simmer for 5 minutes. Put all other ingredients except arrowroot in a milkpan and heat gently until jelly dissolves. Blend the arrowroot with a little water and add to the sauce, stirring until it thickens and clears. Drain the rinds and add to the sauce.

Fruit salad
Serves 8

    3oz (75g) sugar
    8floz (200ml) water
    1 large pineapple, cut into chunks
    4 bananas, thickly sliced
    4 satsumas, segmented
    2 kiwi fruit, sliced
    small melon, cubed or balled
    Maraschino cherries, drained
    miniature favourite liqueur

Dissolve the sugar in the water and then boil for a few minutes until you have a syrup. Cool, then chill. As you prepare the fruit put it into the syrup. Finally add the liqueur and chill for 2 hours.

Christmas Day

Dinner

I never cook anything but dinner on Christmas Day. I find people only want a very light breakfast as they are already looking forward to their lunch!

We always have our dinner at lunchtime and then we have turkey sandwiches and Christmas cake in the evening. I don't believe in the cook washing up either!

I have always preferred a fresh turkey but I know that for some people it is much easier to buy a frozen one. This is quite okay and it is cooked in exactly the same way, the only difference being that care must be taken when defrosting to ensure that the bird is fully thawed before cooking.

Make sure that the bird is kept in a cool place while defrosting. The chart below gives you some idea of how long it will take to defrost and cook your turkey. There is also an indication of how many it will feed. When deciding how many portions you want, allow an extra portion per person for meat for sandwiches, etc. later in the evening or the following day.

Guide to portions and timings

OVEN-READY WEIGHT	PORTIONS	THAWING TIMES	ROUGH GUIDE TO COOKING TIMES
6lb (2.7kg)	8	14 hours	
8lb (3.6kg)	10	16 hours	2-2½ hours
10lb (4.5kg)	12	18 hours	
12lb (5.4kg)	14	20 hours	2¾-3¼ hours
14lb (6.3kg)	16	22 hours	

Cooking times refer to birds, with stuffing, cooked in foil in a pre-heated oven at 220°C/425°F/Gas 7: only a rough guide can be given as all ovens differ.

120

Menu for 8

Prawn and avocado cocktail

Roast turkey and potatoes
Sausages and bacon rolls
Buttered carrots
Brussels sprouts and chestnuts
Cranberry sauce and gravy

Christmas pudding and mince pies
Cream and brandy butter

Time plan: to eat at 1.30

10.00 Stuff turkey and check how long your Christmas pudding takes to re-heat. Some need 3 hours' steaming!
10.15 Pre-heat oven to 220°C/425°F/Gas 7.
10.30 Put turkey in oven. Prepare cranberry sauce and leave to cool. Prepare prawn cocktail mixture and leave to chill. Prepare vegetables and leave in water, prepare and cook chestnuts.
12.30 Parboil potatoes.
12.45 Put potatoes in oven.
 1.20 Take turkey out, put sausages and bacon in oven.
 1.25 Assemble prawn cocktails.
 1.30 Put water on to boil for vegetables, warm plates and serving dishes. Serve prawn cocktails.
 1.40 Put vegetables on to cook, carve turkey.
 1.55 Make gravy.
 2.00 Serve meal.

You will also have to decide when you need to put your pudding on to steam (not forgetting that you will want a rest before you tackle the pudding!). When you put it on depends on how long yours takes to re-heat. Leave the oven on and it will not take long to heat the mince pies when you are ready for them. Don't forget to take the brandy butter out of the refrigerator to let it soften.

Prawn and avocado cocktail
Serves 8

16oz (400g) shelled prawns
1 ripe avocado, de-stoned and cubed
5floz (125ml) mayonnaise
5floz (125ml) tomato sauce
5floz (125ml) single cream
dash Worcester sauce
salt and pepper
Serve with:
shredded lettuce

Mix together the mayonnaise, tomato sauce and cream. Combine with the prawns and avocado; season to taste. Chill until ready to serve. Serve on a bed of shredded lettuce.

Roast turkey
Serves 8   *Pre-heat oven to 220°C/425°F/Gas 7*
(with meat for Boxing Day as well)

stuffing of your choice (page 156)
14lb (6kg) fresh oven-ready turkey
butter

Make up your stuffing or use a ready-made variety. Stuff the NECK end of your turkey. (Make sure the giblets have been removed from body cavity!) Lay foil in your roasting tin and place turkey on this. Spread liberally with butter, then wrap with foil. Roast in the pre-heated oven for 3 hours; 30 minutes before end of cooking time unwrap the foil and baste turkey with buttery juices. Leave foil undone to let turkey get crisp and brown. When a skewer inserted into the thigh produces clear (not pink) juices, the turkey is done. Let the bird rest for at least 15-20 minutes before carving.

Cranberry sauce
Serves 8

8oz (200g) sugar
10floz (250ml) water
1lb (400g) fresh cranberries
1 orange, grated rind and juice
2 tablespoons (30ml) port

Dissolve the sugar in the water over a low heat. Boil for 5 minutes. Add cranberries, orange rind and juice and simmer for 5-10 minutes until cranberries have popped. Add port and mix well. Leave to cool.

Gravy
Serves 8

2 tablespoons (30ml) juices from turkey tin
1 tablespoon (15ml) flour
1 pint (500ml) stock*
2floz (50ml) red wine
1 tablespoon (15ml) cranberry sauce

Put the juices in a pan and sprinkle in the flour, cook over a low heat until beginning to brown. Gradually stir in the stock. Bring to the boil, stirring continuously. Add the wine and sauce and continue to bubble until gravy thickens slightly.

*You could make giblet stock the day before, adding some chopped onion, carrot and celery with a bouquet garni to the water, and simmering for 2 hours before straining.

Brussels sprouts and chestnuts
Serves 8

2lb (800g) Brussels sprouts
1lb (400g) chestnuts*
stock
1 teaspoon (5ml) sugar
knob butter

Remove outer leaves from Brussels sprouts (do not make a cross in the stalk), leave in water while cooking chestnuts. Boil chestnuts for 5 minutes and then while still hot remove shells (this can be painful!). Put shelled chestnuts in a pan with sugar and enough stock to cover and cook for 20 minutes. Drain, cover with clingfilm until ready to use. Cook Brussels sprouts in boiling water for 5-10 minutes. (Do not overcook, or they will go mushy.) Melt butter in a pan, add the chestnuts and coat with butter, mix with sprouts and serve in a warmed serving dish.

*Dried or frozen chestnuts can be substituted for fresh. If using dried, you must pour boiling water over them the day before and leave to soak. Otherwise both dried and frozen chestnuts can be treated as fresh, needing 5-10 minutes to cook.

Sausages and crispy bacon rolls
Serves 8   *Pre-heat oven to 220°C/425°F/Gas 7*

    16 cocktail sausages
    8 rashers streaky bacon, rindless

Put the sausages on a baking tray. Cut rashers across into 2 then roll up and thread on to skewers. Bake in the pre-heated oven for 30-35 minutes until crisp and brown.

Roast potatoes
Serves 8   *Pre-heat oven to 220°C/425°F/Gas 7*

    4lb (1.6kg) potatoes, peeled
    salt and pepper
    beef dripping

Cut the potatoes up into medium chunks. Parboil in a large saucepan for 8 minutes. Drain and season. Heat the fat in a roasting tin and when hot add the potatoes to the pan. Baste with hot fat. Roast for 1¼ hours, turning and basting from time to time. Serve immediately to retain crispness.

Buttered carrots
Serves 8

    2lb (800g) carrots, peeled
    2oz (50g) butter
    chopped fresh parsley

Cut carrots into 2 and then cut into lengths. Bring a pan of water to the boil and add carrots; cook until tender (about 10 minutes) then drain. Melt butter in pan and return carrots to pan, coat thoroughly in butter, sprinkle with chopped parsley and serve in a warmed serving dish.

Boxing Day

Boxing Day is a day of rest for the cook. After the labours of yesterday it is only fair for you to have the chance to put your feet up and take a rest (not literally, as this is a good day to go for a long walk and get some of those calories worked off!). So let someone else cook you a hot breakfast and then endeavour to be in the pub at lunchtime. On returning from their alcoholic lunch everyone will be happy to have a snooze until it is time for afternoon tea. This should consist of muffins and crumpets, served with lashings of butter and a good jam, a piece of Christmas cake (mince pies if you have any left) and a piece of gooey gingerbread. When appetites recover later in the evening, bring out the remains of the turkey, crusty bread and plenty of pickles – that should keep them quiet and complete your rest day!

Gooey gingerbread

Serves 8   *Pre-heat oven to 160°C/325°F/Gas 3*

Make this gingerbread a week in advance so that it goes sticky.

- 1 tablespoon (15ml) golden syrup
- 6 tablespoons (60ml) black treacle
- 3 tablespoons (45ml) muscovado sugar
- 4oz (100g) butter
- 8oz (200g) plain brown flour
- 1 dessertspoon (10ml) baking powder
- 1 teaspoon (5ml) ground ginger
- sprinkling allspice
- 2 eggs, beaten
- ½ teaspoon (3ml) bicarbonate of soda
- 5floz (125ml) milk

Melt the syrup, treacle, sugar and butter over a gentle heat. Sieve all the dry ingredients except bicarbonate of soda and mix with melted mixture. Beat in eggs. Dissolve the bicarbonate of soda in the milk and beat that into the mixture. Line a square 8-inch (20cm) cake tin with greaseproof paper and grease well. Spoon mixture into tin. Bake in the pre-heated oven for 1½ hours or until risen and firm to touch. Cool and peel off paper, cut into squares (will make 9 – so you have 1 for tasting!). Wrap in foil and keep for a week before using.

7. Parties

Most people either love or hate parties and I am presuming that you are in the group that loves 'em, because anyone who considers throwing a party without really loving these occasions must be a masochist!

A party is hard work. Good parties that are enjoyed by everyone must be highly organized, but they are well worth all the trouble. Also most of the work is done in advance so that you as the host are free to enjoy yourself as well.

There are various kinds of party, ranging from affairs where the host provides just a few loaves of bread and a selection of cheeses to occasions where a full buffet meal is served. Most, however, fall somewhere in the middle of these extremes. What you are going to serve depends mainly on why you are holding this party and the numbers you will be inviting.

Whatever sort of party you do decide to hold, always stick to some sort of budget. There is no point in trying to throw a posh cocktail party when you are having to operate on a shoestring. Decide how much you can afford to spend and then plan a party in accordance with this amount.

Basically, however, parties fall into two categories. Finger food, where everything can be eaten with the fingers and therefore there is no need for cutlery and crockery; or fork food, which can be quite simple and is eaten with a fork, usually standing up. Fully fledged buffets for large occasions, which are generally eaten with a knife and fork sitting at a table, are best left to caterers.

I personally always prefer parties that have some sort of theme to them, e.g. Valentine's Day or Hallowe'en. Yet sometimes the feeling just comes over you that this is the right sort of time to have a party. Parties certainly don't need a theme to be successful, but they do need enthusiasm!

If you are going to be busy shopping and preparing all the food for your party, make sure that someone else is organizing the music and sundry items, from seeing that you have enough loo paper on the night to ensuring that there is somewhere for people to put their coats. Don't try to do everything yourself or by the time the party arrives you'll probably be too exhausted to enjoy it properly.

This is certainly where planning comes into its own. Get together with your helper(s) about 1-2 weeks before the event. I suggest you settle down with a bottle of wine to put you in the party spirit, then sort out why you are having this party and who you will invite. Make lists! Then decide who is preparing what. Think through the entire party from the moment the guests arrive until they depart. Next go through the recipes in this section and decide what you will prepare. Don't forget that even if you have decided on a fork affair you may want to provide some finger food for guests who only want to pick. And don't forget the humble crisps and nuts; these are always popular. Finally, make sure you leave plenty of time to get yourself ready. It's your party and you should certainly be the belle (or beau) of the ball!

Depending on the season of your party you will opt for hot or cold food – the problem with hot food being that you cannot totally forget all about it once the party has started, as you will have to serve it at some point. I think hot food should only be attempted for small gatherings, and certainly not for more than 20 friends. The trick is to have one staple food such as potato, rice or pasta and then produce a large casserole dish of food to go with your chosen staple. Make sure you have a couple of salads as well and let people serve themselves. This sort of affair always goes down well for Hallowe'en or Guy Fawkes parties, when the weather is cold and something warm is generally appreciated.

However it is more usual to produce just a few cold dishes which are served with salads, alongside a selection of finger food. This way your guests have the choice of whether they wish to indulge in a full meal or just nibble and of course you, the host, can simply put the food out and then concentrate on enjoying the party!

Finger food

Stuffed vegetable canapés

Celery
Makes 20
>4 celery sticks
>soft cheese, garlic flavoured
>20 fresh chives

Cut each celery stick into 5 equal lengths. Fill the centre grooves with the soft cheese. Tie a chive around the middle of each piece of filled celery.

Courgettes
Makes 20
>10 baby courgettes
>taramasalata
>red lumpfish roe

Cut the ends off the courgettes. Halve lengthways and scoop out the middles. Take a small sliver from the underside of each courgette so that it will stay upright on a plate. Pile some taramasalata into the middle of each and top with some red lumpfish roe.

Mushrooms
Makes 20
>20 small button mushrooms
>soft liver pâté
>small parsley leaves

Remove the stems from the mushrooms. Into the cavity left put a small amount of liver pâté. Top this with a few parsley leaves.

Tomatoes
Makes 20
>20 small cherry tomatoes
>mayonnaise flavoured with tomato purée
>small can of tuna, drained and flaked
>fresh parsley, chopped

Cut the top off each tomato. Scoop out the insides. Mix the mayonnaise with the tuna and use to stuff the tomatoes. Put a little chopped parsley on each and replace the top of the tomato.

Savoury canapés

There are now plenty of products on the supermarket shelves such as pastry cases and crunchy biscuit-type containers that you can use with any of the above stuffings. Just remember not to make them too far in advance so that they do not go soggy. There are also plenty of cocktail biscuits which can be used as a basis for a canapé. Use your favourite brand and spread with one of the following butters or spreads, top with something tasty and you have an elegant canapé. Again do not make too far in advance.

Anchovy butter
4oz (100g) butter, softened
6 anchovies
pimiento-filled green olives

Mash butter and anchovies together and then leave for an hour before using, to let the flavours mingle. After spreading on your biscuits top with a slice of pimiento-filled green olive.

Blue cheese butter
4oz (100g) butter, softened
2oz (50g) Dolcelatte cheese
celery stick

Mix butter and cheese together an hour before using. Then after spreading top with a small slice of celery.

Tomato butter
4oz (100g) butter, softened
1 dessertspoon (10ml) tomato purée
small shelled prawns, fresh or defrosted

Mix the butter and tomato purée and spread on biscuits. Top each with a shelled prawn.

Herb cheese
herb flavoured soft cheese
black lumpfish roe

Spread the cheese on to the biscuits and top with some lumpfish roe.

Garlic cheese
garlic flavoured soft cheese
small slices garlic sausage

Use the cheese to spread on to the biscuits, then quarter each slice of garlic sausage and place a quarter on each biscuit.

Dips

Dips are always popular at parties. Make a selection and surround them with fresh, crunchy vegetables and spicy tortilla crisps.

Garlic and mayonnaise
　　　4oz (100g) soft full fat cheese
　　　2 tablespoons (30ml) mayonnaise
　　　2-3 cloves garlic, crushed or chopped
Blend all ingredients well and pile into a small bowl.

Cheese and onion
　　　4oz (100g) soft full fat cheese
　　　2 tablespoons (30ml) soured cream
　　　spring onions, chopped
Blend together the cheese and soured cream, then add the spring onions until you have the right degree of pungency. Thus this dip can be mild and creamy or thick and oniony!

Chilli and tomato
　　　1 tablespoon (15ml) chilli and tomato relish
　　　1 tablespoon (15ml) tomato purée
　　　1 tablespoon (15ml) olive oil
　　　chilli sauce
Blend the first 3 ingredients and then add chilli sauce to achieve the spiciness that you require.

Avocado
　　　2 very ripe avocados
　　　squeeze of lemon juice
　　　1 clove garlic, crushed or chopped
Cut the avocados in half and scoop ou' the flesh. Mash well with the lemon juice and garlic and pile into a small bowl.

Blue cheese
　　　4oz (100g) blue cheese, crumbled
　　　3 tablespoons (45ml) soured cream
　　　1 tablespoon (15ml) mayonnaise
Blend all ingredients and then pile into a small bowl to serve.

Things-on-sticks

These are always popular. Arrange in circles on round plates or in rows on long plates. Alternatively cut an orange in half and then cover with silver foil; this can then be used to stick the sticks into. Needless to say, all these recipes use cocktail sticks!

The old favourite
    fresh pineapple, cubed
    cocktail onions
    Cheddar cheese, cubed
Thread on to each cocktail stick a piece of pineapple, then a cocktail onion and finally a cube of Cheddar.

You can of course use canned pineapple, but if you try this with fresh pineapple you will never use canned again, as the flavour is vastly superior.

Cheese, tomato and olive sticks
    square cut slices of hard cheese
    stoned black olives
    cherry tomatoes, halved
Cut the cheese slices into triangles. Quarter each olive and thread a piece on to a stick. Follow with a tomato half and then finish with a triangle of cheese.

Brie and black grapes
    Brie, just ripe – not runny
    black grapes
De-rind the Brie and cut cheese into cubes. Halve each grape and remove the pips. Thread half a grape on to a cocktail stick and then a cube of Brie, followed with the second grape half.

Salmon and melon on sticks
        smoked salmon slices
        melon
Cut the salmon into strips about 1 inch long (2.5cm). De-rind and de-seed the melon and cut into small lengths. Wrap a piece of salmon around a piece of melon and spear with a cocktail stick.

Ham and turkey sticks
        slices lean ham
        cooked turkey meat
Cut the ham into thin strips. Cut the turkey into bite-sized pieces. Wrap each turkey piece with a slice of ham. Secure with a cocktail stick.

Posh nibbles ————————————————

Quail's eggs with mock caviar
        quail's eggs, bought ready-cooked
        red lumpfish roe
Carefully shell the eggs and cut each one in half lengthways. Top each with a small amount of lumpfish roe.

Spicy cheese balls
        grated Cheddar cheese
        paprika
Take some cheese and roll into a small ball. Press tightly together and roll in some paprika. Chill for at least 1 hour before serving.

Nutty chicken pieces
        1lb (400g) chicken breasts,   *Pre-heat oven to 200°C/400°F/Gas 6*
            boned and skinned
        4 tablespoons (60ml) crunchy peanut butter
        2 tablespoons (30ml) dark brown sugar
        2 tablespoons (30ml) soy sauce
        2 tablespoons (30ml) lemon juice
Cut up the chicken into bite-sized pieces and marinate in the other ingredients. Leave at least 2 hours, turning every 30 minutes. Place, leaving gaps between each piece, on greased baking trays, and cook in the pre-heated oven for 10 minutes or until the chicken is cooked through. Serve with cocktail sticks which can be used to spear pieces of chicken.

Prawn and sesame triangles

Makes 64   *Pre-heat oven to 200°C/400°F/Gas 6*

8oz (200g) packet shortcrust pastry
1lb (400g) shelled prawns
sprinkling of chilli powder
1 clove garlic, crushed or chopped
2 tablespoons (30ml) tomato purée
1 egg, beaten
sesame seeds

Roll out the pastry to an 16x8-inch (40x20cm) oblong. Finely chop the prawns, add the chilli powder, garlic and tomato purée. Mix well. Brush the pastry with the egg and then add the remaining egg to the prawn mixture. Spread this mixture over the pastry and sprinkle with sesame seeds. Cut into 32 squares. Then cut through each square to make triangles. Place on greased baking trays and cook in the pre-heated oven for 10-15 minutes or until golden brown. Serve cold.

Fork food

Potato panache

Jacket baked potatoes are a useful item when hot food is called for. Allow an 8oz (200g) potato per guest and bake at 200°C/400°F/Gas 6 for 1-1½ hours until potatoes are soft. Serve with 1 of the following fillings.

Cheesy mackerel
    1 pint (500ml) white sauce (page 155)
    4oz (100g) Cheddar cheese, grated
    2 smoked mackerel fillets, flaked
    7-oz (175-g) can sweetcorn, drained
Mix all the ingredients together and heat gently until cheese has melted. (This can be done in a saucepan or in the microwave.)

SOMEBODY LIGHT THE *;-+;. OVEN!

Chilli-chicken
    14-oz (400-g) can chopped tomatoes
    2 cooked chicken breasts, roughly chopped
    1 packet Old El Paso chilli mix
Mix all ingredients and heat gently, stirring well.

Creamed mushrooms
    1lb (400g) mushrooms, sliced
    1 onion, chopped
    1 clove garlic, crushed or chopped
    2oz (50g) butter
    10-oz (250-g) can condensed mushroom soup
    5floz (125ml) soured cream
In a large pan fry the mushrooms, onion and garlic in the butter until soft. Add the soup and cream and heat through.

Rice winners

Another staple that can be served with a big casserole of food is rice. Allow 2oz (50g) rice per person and serve with 1 of the following.

If rice has to be kept hot:
for smallish quantities, place in a strainer covered with a tea towel over a saucepan of gently simmering water, for up to 45 minutes.
for larger quantities, place in a glass dish dotted with butter and covered with foil in a very low oven.
A microwave oven is a useful alternative for reheating.

Chicken curry
Serves 8-10

2 onions, chopped
2 cloves garlic, crushed or chopped
oil for frying
2 tablespoons (30ml) flour
2 tablespoons (30ml) tomato purée
4 tablespoons (60ml) mild curry powder
2 tablespoons (30ml) mango chutney
24oz (600g) cooked chicken, roughly chopped

Fry the onions and garlic in the oil until colouring. Add the remaining ingredients except chicken and blend well. Slowly add 1 pint (500ml) water, stirring continuously. Bring to the boil and then cover and simmer for 25-30 minutes, add the cooked chicken and heat through.

Chilli con carne
Serves 8-10

2 large onions, chopped
2 cloves garlic, crushed or chopped
oil for frying
2lb (800g) minced beef
3 tablespoons (45ml) tomato purée
2 x 14-oz (400-g) cans chopped tomatoes
2 packets Old El Paso chilli mix
2 x 16-oz (400-g) cans kidney beans, drained

Fry the onions and garlic in oil until soft. Then add the meat and cook until brown. Add the rest of ingredients and mix well. Cover and simmer for 2 hours. Keep checking to make sure there is enough liquid in the pan; add water or tomato juice if more liquid is needed.

Party pasta

The other great staple for party dishes is, of course, pasta. Pasta comes in many different colours and shapes. You can serve a colourful dish which consists of a multitude of differing pastas or a single dish of just 1 type. I do think, however, that it is preferable to serve something like 'bows' or 'penne' rather than spaghetti or tagliatelle. Not everyone is an expert spaghetti eater, so do pick a pasta that is easy to eat.

Allow 2-3oz (50g-75g) raw pasta per person and serve with 1 of the following sauces. I always provide freshly grated Parmesan cheese (*YES*, it does taste better) and a big green salad with perhaps a tomato and olive salad.

Abbacchio sauce

Serves 8-10   *Pre-heat oven to 180°C/350°F/Gas 4*

    2lb (800g) lamb fillet, cubed
    1 tablespoon (15ml) butter
    1 tablespoon (15ml) olive oil
    1 large onion, chopped
    3 cloves garlic, crushed or chopped
    1 tablespoon (15ml) flour
    10floz (250ml) dry white wine
    10floz (250ml) chicken stock
    2 lemons, rind and juice
    2 egg yolks
    pinch of dried sage
    salt and pepper
    chopped fresh parsley
    Serve with:
    pasta

Fry the lamb in the butter and oil. Remove lamb from pan and fry the onion and garlic until soft, return lamb to pan. Add flour and stir well. Add wine stock and grated rind of 1 of the lemons. Mix well and transfer to a casserole dish. Cook in the pre-heated oven for 45 minutes. Before serving, beat the egg yolks with the remaining grated lemon rind and the lemon juice, season with sage and salt and pepper and stir into the casserole. Do not return to heat once egg mixture is added. Sprinkle with chopped parsley and serve with pasta.

Bolognese sauce

Serves 8-10

- 2 large onions, chopped
- 2 cloves garlic, crushed or chopped
- 8oz (200g) mushrooms, quartered
- oil for frying
- 1lb (400g) lean minced beef
- 1 tablespoon (15ml) Italian seasoning
- 2 tablespoons (30ml) tomato purée
- splash of red wine
- 2 x 14-oz (400-g) cans tomatoes

Serve with:

- pasta
- grated Parmesan

Fry the onion, garlic and mushrooms in oil until soft. Add the beef and cook until browned. Add the rest of ingredients and bring to boil. Cover and simmer very gently for 45 minutes. Serve with pasta and grated Parmesan.

Vegetarian delights

Of course when cooking for a crowd it can be expensive to provide a meal based on meat. So as an alternative, here are 2 recipes for when you're poverty stricken or for when you need to cater for non-meat eaters.

Tuna and tomato sauce
Serves 8-10

> 3 cloves garlic, crushed or chopped
> 1 tablespoon (15ml) olive oil
> 3 x 14-oz (400-g) cans chopped tomatoes
> 1 tablespoon (15ml) Italian seasoning
> 1 tablespoon (15ml) tomato purée
> 2 x 7-oz (175-g) can tuna, drained
> chopped fresh parsley
> *Serve with:*
> pasta

Fry the garlic in the oil until beginning to brown, add the tomatoes, Italian seasoning and tomato purée. Simmer gently for 15 minutes. Flake the tuna then add to the sauce. Stir well and heat through. Serve with pasta and sprinkle parsley on top.

Creamed mushroom sauce
Serves 8-10

> 8oz (200g) mushrooms, quartered
> 2 tablespoons (30ml) butter
> 2 tablespoons (30ml) olive oil
> dash of mushroom ketchup
> 1 tablespoon (15ml) tomato purée
> 5floz (125ml) dry white wine
> 1 pint (500ml) white sauce (page 155)
> 10floz (250ml) double cream
> salt and pepper
> *Serve with:*
> pasta
> Parmesan cheese

Fry the mushrooms in the butter and oil, until soft. Gradually mix in all other ingredients, stirring well. Season to taste. Serve with pasta and Parmesan cheese.

Cold collation

If you are serving just cold food at your party, then it is a good idea to serve a mixture of cold chicken drumsticks or chicken nuggets (both can be bought ready-cooked), a platter of mixed cold meats, cheeses and a cold quiche. Supply a selection of salads (including 1 made from a staple food) and a few nibbly things.

There are many good quiches on sale in the shops, which are often better than the type a beginner can make at home. However I have included here my favourite party recipe, which is not quite a quiche (it is not pastry based) but more of a savoury cheesecake. Even if you make a couple of these they will disappear very quickly.

Prawn cheesecake
Serves 8-10   *Pre-heat oven to 180°C/350°F/Gas 4*

- 4oz (100g) butter
- 8oz (200g) cheese-flavoured Ritz biscuits, crushed
- 4 tablespoons (120ml) grated Parmesan cheese
- 4oz (100g) full fat cream cheese
- 1 teaspoon (5ml) wholegrain mustard
- 4oz (100g) Gruyère cheese, grated
- 3 eggs, beaten
- 5floz (125ml) soured cream
- 8oz (200g) shelled prawns, chopped
- 1 tablespoon (15ml) spring onions, chopped
- 1 tablespoon (15ml) fresh parsley, chopped

Melt the butter, either in a small saucepan or in the microwave. To this add the crushed biscuits and half the Parmesan. Line an 8-inch (20cm) loose-bottomed flan tin with aluminium foil; into this press the crumb mixture and then chill for 1 hour. Beat the cream cheese with the mustard and remaining cheeses. Gradually stir in the rest of the ingredients. Pile the mixture into the prepared tin, smoothing over the top. Bake in the pre-heated oven for 40-45 minutes or until brown. Chill until ready to serve.

Staple salads

These are quite filling and it is usually only necessary to serve 1 at a time (and not necessary at all if you are serving hot potatoes, rice or pasta).

Potato salad
Serves 8-10

> 2lb (800g) new potatoes, boiled and sliced
> 10floz (250ml) mayonnaise
> spring onions, chopped
> salt and pepper

Mix the potatoes and mayonnaise together, then mix in some spring onions and season to taste.

Brown rice salad
Serves 8-10

> 1lb (400g) brown rice, cooked
> 8-oz (200-g) can pineapple pieces
> 12-oz (300-g) can sweetcorn, drained
> 1 red pepper, de-seeded and chopped
> 2oz (50g) raisins
> nut-flavoured salad dressing (page 168)

Into the cooked rice mix the pineapple, sweetcorn, pepper and raisins. (Use the juices from the pineapple as well.) Then add enough dressing to ensure the salad is thoroughly coated and will not dry out.

Pasta salad
Serves 8-10

> 1lb (400g) pasta bows, cooked
> 6oz (150g) broccoli, cooked and divided into florets
> 6oz (150g) peas, cooked
> a creamy dressing, bought or home-made (blue cheese is nice)

Combine the pasta, broccoli and peas. Use enough dressing to bind the salad together.

Coleslaws

Coleslaws are always popular at parties and I like to include at least 1 type. A coleslaw is based on cabbage, but there are many variations on this theme. Here are some of my most popular coleslaw recipes.

Original coleslaw
Serves 8-10

>1 small white cabbage, finely shredded
>1 large carrot, finely grated
>1 large onion, finely chopped
>10floz (250ml) salad cream or mayonnaise
>lemon juice
>salt and pepper

Combine the cabbage, carrot and onion and bind with as much of the salad cream or mayonnaise as necessary to produce a well-coated salad. Add lemon juice and seasoning to taste. Chill until ready to serve.

To this original mixture can be added any or all of the following:

raisins	caraway seeds
cubed apple	mustard
cubed cheese	curry powder

Redslaw
Serves 8-10

>12oz (300g) red cabbage, finely sliced
>12oz (300g) cooked beetroot, finely grated
>small bunch radishes, sliced
>5floz (125ml) soured cream
>5floz (125ml) mayonnaise

Combine the cabbage, beetroot and radishes. Using as much of the soured cream and mayonnaise as needed, mix the salad together until vegetables are well coated.

Fruitslaw
Serves 8-10

>12oz (300g) white cabbage, finely shredded
>3 celery sticks, thinly sliced
>2 bananas, sliced
>1 apple, cored and sliced
>2 satsumas or tangerines, peeled and segmented
>4oz (100g) seedless white grapes
>10floz (250ml) mayonnaise

Combine all ingredients using as much mayonnaise as necessary.

Mixed salads

Tomato and olive salad
Serves 8-10
> 2lb (800g) fresh tomatoes, sliced
> handful of stoned black olives
> 1 tablespoon (15ml) chopped fresh chives
> virgin olive oil

Lay the sliced tomatoes in a shallow dish, quarter the olives and scatter over the tomatoes. Sprinkle with the chives and finally drizzle with the olive oil. Leave at least 1 hour before serving.

Mushroom salad
Serves 8-10
> 12oz (300g) mushrooms, quartered
> oil for frying
> 1 teaspoon (5ml) curry powder
> 5floz (125ml) Greek cows' yoghurt
> lemon juice

Fry the mushrooms in the oil and curry powder until soft. Drain and then mix with the yoghurt. Add lemon juice to taste. Chill for at least 1 hour.

Waldorf salad
Serves 8-10
> 4 red apples, cored and sliced
> 2 tablespoons (30ml) lemon juice
> 4 celery sticks, finely sliced
> 8oz (200g) shelled walnuts, chopped
> 12floz (300ml) mayonnaise
> salt and pepper

Combine all ingredients and chill.

Green party salad
Serves 8-10
> 1 large Cos or Webb's lettuce, shredded
> punnet of cress
> ½ cucumber, thinly sliced
> 1 green pepper, de-seeded and chopped
> French dressing (page 167)

Combine all salad ingredients and just before people arrive drizzle liberally with dressing.

Party drinks

More often than not hosts provide a few bottles of wine and a few beers and ask their guests to 'bring a bottle'. However there are some occasions when even if you are asking your guests to contribute, it should be up to you, the host, to provide a special drink. For instance, in the summer a wine cup may be the perfect drink to offer your guests on arrival. Or in the winter months, especially for Hallowe'en or Guy Fawkes, it is nice to offer your guests some mulled wine to help keep out the cold! In drinks which generally use champagne you could try substituting a very good dry sparkling wine like Veuve du Vernay or sparkling Saumur. They are almost indistinguishable when mixed in drinks and are half the price of champagne.

Wine-based cold drinks————————————

Wine cup
    1 bottle red wine
    1 bottle white wine
    miniature brandy or Cointreau
    30floz (750ml) lemonade
    strawberries, sliced
    ice

Mix the wines, brandy and lemonade together and chill for at least 1 hour. Just before serving add the strawberries and ice.

Bucks fizz
    orange juice
    1 bottle champagne
    ice

Quarter fill a glass or large jug with orange juice and ice. Top up with champagne.

Bellini

    mango or apricot juice
    champagne

Fill champagne flute one-third full with juice and then top up with champagne.

Champagne cocktail

    sugar cubes
    angostura bitters
    champagne

Put a sugar cube in the bottom of a champagne glass. Put 1-2 drops angostura bitters on to sugar and fill glass with champagne.

Kir

    1 dessertspoon (10ml) crème de cassis
    dry white wine

Put crème de cassis into champagne flute and then top up with wine.

Note: To make a Kir Royale, substitute champagne for the white wine.

Hot drinks

Mulled wine
>1 bottle red wine
>10floz (250ml) dry cider
>1 tablespoon (15ml) port
>1 tablespoon (15ml) brandy
>2 cinnamon sticks
>4 cloves
>sprinkling of mace
>3 tablespoons (45ml) honey
>3 tablespoons (45ml) orange juice
>1 orange, sliced
>1 lemon, sliced

Put all ingredients into a large saucepan and heat gently until honey has melted and mixture is warmed through. Do not allow to boil. (You can also microwave this: cook for 8 minutes and then leave to stand for 5 minutes.)

Note: A useful tip here is to keep the mulled wine warm in a coffee maker while you are drinking some of it. Just put it in the jug, switch on the machine and place the jug on the warm plate.

Hot buttered toddies
Per person
>cup of milk
>2 tablespoons (30ml) rum
>1 teaspoon (5ml) sugar
>knob of butter

Gently heat the milk, but do not boil. When warmed through add the rum and sugar and stir well. Pour into mug and top with a knob of butter. A drink to keep out the winter chill!

Irish coffee
Per person
>2 tablespoons (30ml) Irish whiskey
>1 teaspoon (5ml) sugar
>cup hot fresh coffee
>double cream

Put the whiskey and sugar into the bottom of a heat-proof glass, add the coffee and stir until sugar is dissolved. Pour the cream slowly over the back of a spoon so that it floats on the coffee. Serve immediately.

Cocktails

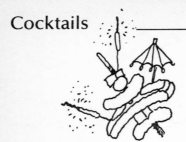

Cocktails are always fun to drink and make. One word of warning, though, if holding a cocktail party. Do make sure that you will have plenty of help on the night and stick to making just a few cocktails.

Draw pictures of the cocktails you will be making with a list of their ingredients underneath. Put on the wall, these make good decorations *AND* ensure that your helpers know how to make the cocktail! Finally, ensure that you have plenty of ice, cocktail parasols and fruit garnishes – a cocktail isn't the same without these fancy bits and pieces.

Note: 1 measure = 2 tablespoons (30ml)

Martini

    ice
    2 measures gin
    1 measure dry vermouth
    Serve with:
    stuffed olive and a knot of lemon peel

Put ice into a mixing glass and add gin and vermouth. Stir until ice begins to melt. Strain into a cocktail glass and add olive and lemon peel.

Between-the-sheets

    1 measure rum
    1 measure brandy
    1 measure Cointreau
    1 measure lemon juice
    ice
    Serve with:
    twist of lemon

Put all ingredients into a cocktail shaker; shake. Strain into a cocktail glass. Decorate with a twist of lemon.

Brandy Alexander
>1 measure brandy
>1 measure Tia Maria
>1 measure cream
>ice
>*Serve with:*
>sprinkling of grated nutmeg

Put all ingredients in a cocktail shaker; shake. Strain into a cocktail glass and sprinkle with a little nutmeg.

The ultimate drink must be the Mai-tai but be warned – it is very potent!

Mai-tai
>ice
>2 measures white rum
>1 measure rum
>1 measure tequila
>1 measure Cointreau
>orange juice
>dash of grenadine
>*Serve with:*
>fresh fruit garnish

Put the ice into a long straight glass, add the rums, tequila and Cointreau. Top up with orange juice, add a dash of grenadine and stir well. Garnish with plenty of fresh fruit.

Black Russian
    ice
    2 measures vodka
    1 measure Tia Maria
    Coca-Cola
Put ice into a long glass, add vodka and Tia Maria, stir. Top up with Coca-Cola.

Tequila sunrise
    ice
    1 measure tequila
    orange juice
    1 teaspoon (5ml) grenadine
    Serve with:
    orange slice and cocktail cherries
Put the ice into a long glass. Add the tequila and fill up with orange juice; stir. Add the grenadine – DO NOT STIR. Decorate and serve.

Harvey Wallbanger
    ice
    1 measure vodka
    orange juice
    1 measure Galliano
    Serve with:
    slice of orange
Put ice into a long straight glass. Add vodka and fill up with orange juice; stir. Add Galliano slowly, so that most of it floats on top. Decorate with orange.

Freddy Fudpucker
As for Harvey Wallbanger, but substituting tequila for the vodka.

Of course many people's favourite cocktail is the Pina colada. There are many variations of this recipe, but this is a very good one.

Pina colada

    ice

    2 measures white rum

    2 measures coconut cream *or* 1 measure Malibu and 1 measure cream

    pineapple juice

    Serve with:

    fresh pineapple garnish and cocktail cherries

Put all ingredients in a blender and blend quickly. Strain into a bulb cocktail glass and garnish with pineapple and cherries.

8. Serve with. . .

Whenever you pick out a menu for a dinner party you have to decide on what accompaniments to serve with the main course. For most recipes I have suggested ideas of things to serve with them. However it may be that you want to serve fresh vegetables and what I have suggested is not in season when you come to serve a particular dish. So in this section I have given a selection of vegetable and salad dishes that can be served alongside your main course.

I have also included some basic sauces and other items, such as Yorkshire pudding, that it is useful to know how to make. Within this section you will also find guidance on quantities for pasta, rice and potatoes.

Basic recipes

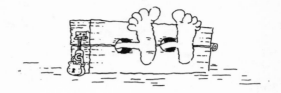

Stock

Although I have used stock in recipes throughout this book I have not specified whether this is home-made or made from a stock cube. This is because I know that most people do not have the time to make their own stock. However it is very easy to make and well worthwhile, as it really does add a little special something to the finished dish. I am very lazy when making stock. Basically I just put my roast chicken or roasted meat bones in a large pan, cover with water and add a few bay leaves. Then I cover, bring to the boil and simmer for 1 hour. I drain the resulting liquid into a bowl and leave overnight in the fridge. It then jells and I can easily skim off any fat. I then re-boil the stock and simmer until the liquid is reduced by half. This I cool and pour into an ice cube maker to freeze. The resulting stock cubes I bag up and label with the date made. Then, whenever I need some stock, I have some ready-made in the freezer.

If all this seems like too much hassle you can use a good brand of stock cubes to make your stock. You usually need 1 stock cube per 15floz (375ml) water.

Another alternative to home-made stock or the stock cube is a can of good consommé. This is a clear soup that is basically a concentrated stock. You can find it in beef or game flavour, and it makes a very acceptable alternative to stock.

Gravy

Quite often at home I resort to a packet mix for the gravy for the Sunday roast. This saves having to make the gravy at the last moment and often has a lot less calories than the sort of gravy you generally make at home, where you add juices from the meat. If, however, you are not worried about its calorie count and want to make authentic gravy, this is how it's done.

Once the meat has been removed from the roasting tin, drain off all but 2 tablespoons (30ml) of the fat, sprinkle in 1 tablespoon (15ml) flour and blend well. Add a little of the water you have cooked the vegetables in (or a little stock) and mix well. Return the tin to the heat and, stirring well, gradually add enough vegetable water or stock to make a gravy of your required thickness. Add a little gravy browning for extra colour. Serve very hot.

Sauces

White sauce

A white sauce is used as the basic sauce in many dishes. Although you can buy a packet mix this is a very easy sauce to make, even for a beginner.

However much sauce you want to make, the basic proportion is always the same. 1oz (25g) butter to 1oz (25g) flour and 10floz (250ml) milk. A rounded tablespoon of flour is equivalent to 1oz (25g) flour.

To make the sauce: Melt the butter in a saucepan. Remove from the heat and beat in the flour. Add a little of the milk and blend into the sauce. Return to the heat and gradually add the rest of the milk, stirring well. If the sauce appears to be going lumpy, remove from the heat and beat fiercely. When smooth again return to heat and carry on adding the milk. When all the milk has been added simmer for a few minutes and season with a little salt and pepper. This sauce can be enriched with cream or made into cheese sauce.

Cheese sauce

To the basic white sauce mix made with 10floz (250ml) milk, add 2oz (50g) grated strong-flavoured cheese and 1 teaspoon (5ml) wholegrain mustard. Mix well and cook until cheese has melted into sauce.

Mushroom sauce

Add 4oz (100g) sliced mushrooms and 1 tablespoon (15ml) double cream to a basic white sauce made with 10floz (250ml) milk.

Cheats mushroom sauce

        8oz (200g) mushrooms, sliced
        1oz (25g) unsalted butter
        2 tablespoons (30ml) tomato purée
        12-oz (300-g) can condensed mushroom soup
        2 tablespoons (30ml) red wine

Fry mushrooms in butter until soft. Add rest of ingredients and simmer for 5 minutes.

Apple sauce

   16oz (400g) cooking apples, peeled, cored and sliced
   1oz (25g) unsalted butter
   sugar

Put the apples in a saucepan with 3 tablespoons (45ml) water. Simmer for 10 minutes until apples are soft. Beat to a purée or purée in a blender. Return to heat and add butter. Heat until butter melts. Stir well and add sugar to taste.

Mint sauce

Many of us make the mint sauce for our lamb with the mint sauce mixes that are found in every supermarket. However if you do have some fresh mint and want to make your own sauce this is how to do it.

   Take a small bunch of mint and wash and chop it finely, discarding the stalks. Put in a sauce boat and add 1 tablespoon (15ml) sugar. Add a little boiling water and stir until the sugar has dissolved. Add 1-2 tablespoons (15-30ml) vinegar to taste. Leave to cool before serving.

Accompaniments _____

Sage and onion stuffing

   2 large onions, chopped
   1oz (25g) butter, softened
   4oz (100g) fresh breadcrumbs
   2 teaspoons (10ml) dried sage
   salt and pepper

Boil the onions in water until soft. Drain and add rest of ingredients. Season to taste. Use to stuff chicken or put in a greased foil tray and bake at 200°C/400°F/Gas 6 for 20-30 minutes or until brown and crispy on top.

   You can vary the above recipe in many ways. By adding some chopped mushrooms and walnuts and a tablespoon (15ml) cider you will make a MUSHROOM AND WALNUT STUFFING for pork. You can add grated orange or lemon rind and 1 tablespoon (15ml) juice with a sprinkling of raisins for a FRUIT AND RAISIN STUFFING. Chopped celery and apple also makes a good addition. I'm sure you can think of plenty of different ways of making it, varying the herbs used and using small amounts of fruit, vegetables and flavourings such as cider, wine or fruit juices.

Yorkshire pudding

4oz (100g) flour
pinch of salt
1 egg, beaten
10floz (250ml) milk
dripping, lard or oil

Pre-heat oven to 220°C/425°F/Gas 7

Sift the flour and salt into a mixing bowl. Make a well in the centre of the flour and pour in the egg and half the milk. Draw the flour into the liquid and mix until a thick batter is formed. Gradually beat in the rest of the milk. Put a little fat into each of the holes in a 12-hole bun tin or 4-hole Yorkshire pudding tin. Put the tin into the oven for a few minutes to heat the fat. Fill the holes in the tin with the batter. Cook in the pre-heated oven for 20 minutes or until the puddings are risen and brown.

Potatoes

Potatoes are very popular as an accompaniment to the main course. In the summer new potatoes are a lovely accompaniment to most dinner party dishes, while in the winter a cooked potato dish is always welcome. If preparation time is short, jacket baked potatoes are a good choice and Sunday lunch wouldn't be the same without roast potatoes. Although the trend in recent years has been towards healthier ways of serving our meals, roast potatoes are still a vice of mine. I don't think you can beat chunks of crisp tasty roast potatoes – even if they are calorie-laden!

New potatoes

Allow 4-6oz (100-150g) per person. Do not peel. Put into boiling water and cook until just tender. There are many varieties on the market, so only a rough guide to their cooking time can be given. Roughly the smaller and younger the potato the shorter the cooking time required. Some will be ready in 8 minutes, others will take up to 15 minutes. Generally, the smaller they are the better the flavour. Serve seasoned with salt and pepper and with a knob of butter.

Roast potatoes

Allow 6-8oz (150-200g) per person. Peel and cut into medium chunks. Parboil for 5 minutes, season with salt and pepper and then cook in a roasting tin in dripping, lard or oil at 200°C/400°F/Gas 6 for 1¼-1½ hours, basting and turning occasionally.

Jacket baked potatoes

Allow 6-8oz (150-200g) potato per person. Cook in a pre-heated oven at 200°C/400°F/Gas 6 for 1-1½ hours until potato is soft inside. Either serve in a serving bowl and let people choose their own, and put butter or soured cream on the table, or cut a cross in the top of each potato, give a slight squeeze so that the potato inside shows and put a knob of butter on this, then serve individually.

Potatoes au gratin

Serves 4   *Pre-heat oven to 180°C/350°F/Gas 4*

 1lb (400g) old potatoes, peeled
 5floz (125ml) single cream
 salt and pepper
 1 tablespoon (15ml) fresh breadcrumbs
 2oz (50g) cheese, grated

Boil the potatoes for 5 minutes and then put into cold water. When cool enough to handle, slice thinly. Put into a buttered ovenproof dish. Season the cream with salt and pepper and then pour over the potato. Mix the breadcrumbs and cheese and sprinkle over the top. Bake in the pre-heated oven for 45 minutes or until brown and crispy.

Pasta

Pasta is a very versatile ingredient in the busy cook's repertoire. It can be bought in many varieties in both its dried and fresh forms. In its fresh form it is extremely quick to cook, taking literally just a few minutes. In its dried form it varies from 8 minutes to 12 minutes to cook. Whichever type of pasta you buy will come with its recommended cooking time on the packaging, so if transferring the contents to a pretty pasta jar, remember to make a note of how long the contents take to cook!

People do vary in how much pasta they can eat. Generally allow 2-4oz (50-100g) per person. I always allow 4oz (100g) for a dish like bows when serving with a casserole, but only 2oz (50g) tagliatelle when serving as a side dish at a formal dinner party. Allow 1oz (25g) more per person when serving fresh pasta. To cook, place pasta in boiling water and cook for required length of time. Drain, add a knob of butter and season well with freshly ground black pepper. Depending on what you are serving it with you could toss in some grated Parmesan cheese or chopped parsley.

Tagliatelle with sesame seeds
Serves 4
This is a favourite dinner-party dish of mine.

> 8oz (200g) mixed spinach and egg tagliatelle
> large knob of butter
> sprinkling of sesame seeds
> 1 tablespoon (15ml) single cream
> salt and pepper

Cook the tagliatelle, drain. Melt butter and add sesame seeds, quickly stir fry then add cream, warm through and mix with tagliatelle. Season with salt and pepper; serve immediately.

Rice

Rice is a useful dish to serve at a dinner party because once cooked it can be kept warm in a cool oven until ready to serve. Some people worry about using rice because they have found that it sticks together and comes out in a blob. If this happens to you, change your type of rice! If you use a good quality rice, you just shouldn't have this sort of problem. Always use a long grain variety; the best is usually basmati, now available in both white and brown. Which one you use of course depends on your own taste. Again, different varieties need different cooking times so take a note of the manufacturer's recommended cooking time. Allow 2-3oz (50-75g) per person.

To cook, place in a saucepan and cover with twice the rice's volume of water or stock. Bring to the boil, cover and simmer for the recommended time. Do not stir the rice. When cooked and water has been absorbed, turn off heat and leave for a few minutes before forking up and serving. If there is any water still left at the end of the cooking time, and the rice is cooked, drain and put into a heatproof dish. Cover and leave in a cool oven for 10 minutes.

Fruit pilaff
Serves 4

> 8oz (200g) basmati rice
> 20floz (500ml) chicken stock
> 2oz (50g) unsalted butter
> 2oz (50g) raisins
> 2oz (50g) no-soak dried apricots, chopped
> sprinkling of paprika
> salt and pepper

Cook the basmati in the stock until cooked. Drain. Melt the butter and quickly stir fry the raisins and apricots with the paprika. Add to rice, season and put into a buttered ovenproof dish. Cover and put in a cool oven for 30 minutes. Fork up before serving.

Petits pois à la Française
Serves 4
>8oz (200g) frozen petits pois
>1 onion, chopped
>2oz (50g) butter
>2 lettuce leaves, finely shredded
>salt and pepper

Cook the peas in boiling water, drain. Fry the onion in the butter until brown. Add the lettuce leaves and quickly stir fry. Add the peas, season and serve immediately.

Creamed leeks
Serves 4
>4 leeks, trimmed and sliced
>2oz (50g) butter
>1 teaspoon (5ml) wholegrain mustard
>2 tablespoons (30ml) single cream
>salt and pepper

Fry the leeks in the butter until soft. Add the mustard and cream and simmer until cream is warmed through, season and serve immediately.

Leeks Provençale
Serves 4
>4 leeks, trimmed and sliced
>2 tablespoons (30ml) olive oil
>2 cloves garlic, crushed or chopped
>7-oz (200-g) can chopped tomatoes
>splash of red wine
>chopped parsley

Fry the leeks in the oil until soft. Add garlic and tomatoes and quickly stir fry. Add a splash of red wine and serve sprinkled with chopped parsley. This dish can be left covered in a cool oven until ready to serve.

Broccoli
Serves 4
>1½lb (600g) fresh broccoli, trimmed

Divide broccoli into florets, put into boiling water and cook for 8-10 minutes, until tender but still with 'bite'. The broccoli florets can also be cooked in a metal colander over boiling water, but they will take longer to cook.

Glazed carrots
Serves 4

    2oz (50g) butter
    1lb (400g) baby carrots
    1 tablespoon (15ml) caster sugar
    home-made beef stock or consommé
    chopped parsley

Melt the butter, add the carrots, sugar and enough stock or consommé to half-cover the carrots. Cook gently until carrots are tender. Remove carrots and boil the liquid until reduced to a syrupy glaze. Return the carrots to the pan and coat thoroughly. Serve sprinkled with parsley.

Glazed turnips
Serves 4

    1lb (400g) baby turnips, sliced
    2oz (50g) butter
    1 tablespoon (15ml) brown sugar
    1 tablespoon (15ml) reduced stock or consommé

Fry the turnips in the butter until tender and beginning to brown. Add the sugar and stock, stir while frying. When syrupy glaze has thoroughly coated turnips, serve immediately.

French beans with almonds
Serves 4

    1lb (400g) fresh French beans
    2oz (50g) flaked almonds
    knob of butter

Cook the French beans in boiling salted water for 10-12 minutes until tender but still with some 'bite'. Grill the almonds, watching carefully as they burn very easily. Add the butter to the beans and coat the beans thoroughly. Mix with the almonds and serve immediately.

Raisined cabbage
Serves 4

½ Savoy cabbage, finely shredded
2oz (50g) butter
gurgle of white wine
2oz (50g) raisins
salt and pepper

Place butter in the bottom of a saucepan and then put cabbage on top. Pour in the wine, sprinkle with raisins. Cover and cook for 5-10 minutes until butter is absorbed and wine has evaporated. Season before serving.

Button mushrooms
Serves 4

1lb (400g) button mushrooms
1 clove garlic, crushed or chopped
2oz (50g) butter
chopped parsley
salt and pepper

Quickly fry the mushrooms and garlic in the butter. Remove from heat, sprinkle with parsley and season. Mix well and serve immediately.

Nutty spinach
Serves 4

1lb (400g) spinach leaves, shredded
salt and pepper
2oz (50g) cashew nuts
sprinkling of mustard seeds

Boil a pan of water. Add spinach and turn heat off. Leave 5 minutes. Drain, season to taste and sprinkle with cashews and mustard seed.

Parsnip purée
Serves 4

1lb parsnips, finely sliced
1oz (75g) butter
1 tablespoon (15ml) single cream
squeeze of lemon juice
salt and pepper

Boil the parsnips until tender, drain. Mash well or purée in a blender with butter, cream and lemon juice. Season to taste before serving. Can be piled into an ovenproof dish, covered and left in a cool oven until ready to serve.

Roast parsnips

Serves 4   *Pre-heat oven to 200°C/400°F/Gas 6*

> 1lb (400g) parsnips, quartered
> 2oz (50g) butter
> 1 tablespoon (15ml) clear honey
> salt and pepper
> sprinkling of sesame seeds (optional)

Boil the parsnips in water for 10 minutes. Drain and put into a small roasting tin with butter. Pour honey over parsnips and season. Bake in the pre-heated oven for 20 minutes, turning occasionally. If using sesame seeds, sprinkle them over the parsnips 5 minutes before the end of their cooking time.

Courgettes with lemon

Serves 4

> 1lb courgettes, sliced
> 2oz (50g) butter
> sprinkling of chopped chives
> squeeze of lemon juice
> salt and pepper

Fry the courgettes in the butter until tender and add chives, lemon juice and salt and pepper to taste. Can be left covered in the pan and re-heated quickly just before serving.

Courgettes with tomatoes

Serves 4

> 1lb (400g) courgettes, sliced
> 2 cloves garlic, crushed or chopped
> 2 tablespoons (30ml) olive oil
> 7-oz (200-g) can chopped tomatoes
> sprinkling of chopped parsley

Fry the courgettes and garlic in the oil until courgettes are tender. Add the tomatoes and simmer for a few minutes to let the flavours mingle. Sprinkle with chopped parsley before serving. This dish can be left, covered, in a cool oven until ready to serve.

Cauliflower cheese

Serves 4   *Pre-heat oven to 200°C/400°F/Gas 6*

    1 small cauliflower, trimmed and divided into florets
    1½oz (40g) butter
    1½oz (40g) flour
    10floz (250ml) milk
    1 teaspoon (5ml) wholegrain mustard
    4oz (100g) cheese, grated
    salt and pepper
    2 tablespoons (30ml) fresh breadcrumbs

Cook the cauliflower in boiling water for 7 minutes or until just tender. Melt the butter, remove from heat and beat in flour and a little of the milk. Return to heat and, while stirring, gradually add the rest of the milk. When you have a thick sauce add the mustard and three quarters of the cheese. Mix well and season. Put the cauliflower into a buttered ovenproof dish, pour the cheese sauce over. Mix the remaining cheese with the breadcrumbs and sprinkle on top of the cauliflower cheese. Bake in the pre-heated oven for 20-30 minutes until brown. Alternatively you can put under a hot grill until crispy and brown.

Salads

At a dinner party it is often preferable to serve a salad instead of vegetables with the main course. The salad and its dressing can be prepared before your guests arrive and then the salad only needs to be dressed just before serving. Especially when some of the courses have been very rich, salads can be very refreshing to the palate and they don't have to be reserved for summer: a salad is just as welcome in the colder months.

A salad can be as formal or informal as you like. I like to serve my salads in a lovely glass salad bowl. However they can also be served in separate bowls or on side plates, one to each diner. The artichoke and mange-tout salad is an elegant dinner-party dish that is particularly suited to serving in individual portions.

Green salad
Serves 4

> 3 varieties green-leaved lettuce
> cress
> ½ cucumber, thinly sliced
> 1 kiwi fruit, peeled and sliced
> 1 green pepper, de-seeded, chopped
> *Serve with:*
> a dressing of your choice

Allow a handful of lettuce leaves per person, shred and put in a serving bowl, add rest of ingredients and cover and chill. Dress with your chosen dressing just before serving.

Mixed salad
Serves 4

> 1 red-leaved variety of lettuce
> 1 green-leaved variety of lettuce
> 4oz (100g) red cabbage, finely sliced
> 1 carrot, grated
> 12 cherry tomatoes or 4 tomatoes, quartered
> *Serve with:*
> a dressing of your choice

Using a handful of leaves for each person, line a serving bowl with lettuce. Add rest of ingredients. Cover and chill. Using your chosen dressing, dress just before serving.

Broccoli and avocado salad
Serves 4

6oz (150g) fresh broccoli, trimmed and divided into florets
2 gem lettuces, roughly shredded
1 large ripe avocado, de-stoned and sliced lengthways
squeeze of lemon juice
sprinkling of pumpkin seeds
Serve with:
a dressing of your choice

Place broccoli in boiling water and simmer for 3 minutes. Drain and leave to cool. Arrange lettuce in serving bowl, add cooled broccoli and avocado and sprinkle with lemon juice. Cover and chill. Just before serving dress with chosen dressing and sprinkle with pumpkin seeds.

Artichoke and mange-tout salad
Serves 4

16-oz (400-g) can artichoke hearts
3 tablespoons (45ml) olive oil
squeeze of lemon juice
8oz (200g) mange-tout
freshly ground black pepper

Drain artichokes and cut each heart into 4. Place in a serving bowl and add olive oil and lemon juice. Mix to coat thoroughly. Cover and chill. Cook mange-tout for 2 minutes and then put into cold water. Drain and chill until ready to serve. Just before serving mix mange-tout with artichokes and sprinkle with black pepper.

Salad dressings

French dressing
Serves 4

1 teaspoon (5ml) wholegrain mustard
2 tablespoons (30ml) olive oil
1 tablespoon (15ml) wine vinegar
salt and pepper
sprinkling of chopped fresh or dried herbs

Put all ingredients into a container with a lid and shake vigorously. The dressing will separate as it stands, so mix again before serving.

Nut dressing
Serves 4

> 2 tablespoons (30ml) sesame, hazelnut or walnut oil
> 1 tablespoon (15ml) lemon juice
> salt and pepper
> sprinkling of chopped nuts
> sprinkling of sesame seeds

Put the oil, lemon juice and salt and pepper into a container with a lid and shake vigorously. Before serving add the nuts and sesame seeds.

Lime dressing
Serves 4

> 1 lime, grated rind and 1 tablespoon (15ml) juice
> 1 tablespoon (15ml) olive oil
> 3 tablespoons (45ml) single cream
> salt and pepper

Put all ingredients into a container with a lid. Shake well and chill before serving.

Creamy nut dressing
Serves 4

> 1 tablespoon (15ml) sesame oil
> 1 teaspoon (5ml) wholegrain mustard
> 1 teaspoon (5ml) clear honey
> salt and pepper
> 3 tablespoons (45ml) single cream

Put all ingredients in a container with a lid. Shake vigorously and chill before serving.

Index

Notes

Notes

Notes

Notes